Jane Froman

4|06
Un. Mo Press
11.65
Lib|TI

Project Sponsors

Missouri Center for the Book
Western Historical Manuscript Collection,
    University of Missouri–Columbia

Special Thanks

Claudia Powell, Graphic Specialist,
    Western Historical Manuscript Collection,
    University of Missouri–Columbia
Suzanna Grenz
David Sapp
A. E. Schroeder
Judie Wright

Missouri Heritage Readers

General Editor, Rebecca B. Schroeder

Each Missouri Heritage Reader explores a particular aspect of the state's rich cultural heritage. Focusing on people, places, historical events, and the details of daily life, these books illustrate the ways in which people from all parts of the world contributed to the development of the state and the region. The books incorporate documentary and oral history, folklore, and informal literature in a way that makes these resources accessible to all Missourians.

Intended primarily for adult new readers, these books will also be invaluable to readers of all ages interested in the cultural and social history of Missouri.

Books in the Series

Blind Boone: Missouri's Ragtime Pioneer, by Jack A. Batterson

Called to Courage: Four Women in Missouri History, by Margot Ford McMillen and Heather Roberson

Food in Missouri: A Cultural Stew, by Madeline Matson

German Settlement in Missouri: New Land, Old Ways, by Robyn K. Burnett and Ken Luebbering

Jesse James and the Civil War in Missouri, by Robert L. Dyer

On Shaky Ground: The New Madrid Earthquakes of 1811–1812, by Norma Hayes Bagnall

Orphan Trains to Missouri, by Michael D. Patrick and Evelyn Goodrich Trickel

The Osage in Missouri, by Kristie C. Wolferman

Paris, Tightwad, and Peculiar: Missouri Place Names, by Margot Ford McMillen

Quinine and Quarantine: Missouri Medicine through the Years, by Loren Humphrey

The Trail of Tears across Missouri, by Joan Gilbert

Jane Froman

- missouri's

- first lady

- of song

Ilene Stone

UNIVERSITY OF MISSOURI PRESS • Columbia and London

University of Missouri Press, Columbia, Missouri 65201
Printed and bound in the United States of America
5 4 3 2 1   07 06 05 04 03

Library of Congress Cataloging-in-Publication Data

Stone, Ilene, 1945–
  Jane Froman : Missouri's first lady of song / Ilene Stone.
    p. cm.
Includes bibliographical references, discography, and
filmography (p.), and index.
  ISBN 0-8262-1458-4
  1. Froman, Jane, 1907–1980. 2. Singers—United States—
Biography. I.
Title.
  ML420.F866 S76 2003
  782.42164'092—dc21

                                        2002154944

∞™ This paper meets the requirements of the
American National Standard for Permanence of Paper
for Printed Library Materials, Z39.48, 1984.

Designer: Liz Young
Typesetter: Foley Design
Printer and binder: Thomson-Shore, Inc.
Typefaces: Cushing Book, Weissach, Poppl-Exquisit Regular

To my husband Jeff,

with gratitude and love for his constant patience,

his strong support, and for always being there for me.

Contents

Preface

Several years ago, finding myself with a little time to relax, and liking old motion pictures, musicals in particular, I came across a movie on television that I thought would be interesting. *With a Song in My Heart* starred Susan Hayward in the story of a singer and entertainer named Jane Froman— someone I was not familiar with. The movie greatly affected me. In fact, it changed my life, sending me on a mission to learn more about the film's intriguing subject.

The 1952 movie, which is labeled a "biopic," in reality deals with only a short period in Jane Froman's life. It briefly covers her early career and rise to prominence as one of America's top female performers prior to World War II. The main emphasis of the picture, however, is on the injuries she sustained in 1943 when her USO plane crashed into the Tagus River near Lisbon, Portugal, and her subsequent valiant efforts to regain her health and reestablish her career. It makes no attempt to define who the real Jane Froman was or to explore how she found the strength to cope with all that came her way. The film does not treat many aspects of Jane's life, though it does showcase her marvelous voice through the art of dubbing.

I was left with many questions, including what had happened to Jane Froman after 1945, when the movie story ends. I went to the library in search of a book about her but learned that there was no Froman memoir, no full-length biography. I soon discovered that the only way to find out more about her life was to search through books in which she was briefly mentioned, to read the various magazines of her time, and to spend hours in front of a microfilm reader scanning newspaper stories. All of these pursuits proved unsatisfactory and unfulfilling. The facts had not been brought together in one place—the life story of the gallant woman depicted in the film was not available.

My research soon led me to Columbia, Missouri, a place that was important to me for three reasons. Not only was it Jane's hometown, but the Jane Froman Papers are housed and cataloged at the Western Historical Manuscript Collection at the University of Missouri–Columbia. Third, and more important for my research, there were other materials at the Walters–Boone County Historical Museum and at Columbia College. It was at the college that I found a copy of Jane's notes for an unpublished autobiography that she called "Time to Go Home." There are other Froman memorabilia there as well, including her baby book.

Jane started to write her life story sometime in 1964 or 1965, but she never finished it. While it is only an outline, especially for the years after 1943, it is nevertheless a treasure trove of information about her family, her early life, and her career. It reveals, to some extent, the kind of person she was and the experiences that shaped her.

Since my discovery of "Time to Go Home," I have written several pieces about Jane. These include a privately published partial biography, *One Little Candle: Remembering Jane Froman,* which I coauthored with Suzanna Grenz and which details Jane's retirement years; a biographical sketch for the *Dictionary of Missouri Biography;* and an essay in the book *Boone County Chronicles* about Jane's efforts to sell World War II bonds in Columbia. Over time, these projects required that I try to locate and study all the available research materials about Jane Froman: her papers, her correspondence, photographs of her, newspaper stories, magazine articles (some of which she wrote herself), fan journals, microfilm of her scrapbooks, letters that others wrote about her, and various county and state records relating to her and her family. I listened to her recordings, watched episodes of her television show and other programs in which she appeared, and talked to people who knew her. Her friends and acquaintances gave generously of their time to share their memories of Jane with me through letters, phone interviews, and one-on-one conversations.

For this book, in addition to Jane's unpublished autobiography, I used two other important documents. One is a letter of September 23, 1950, from a Froman cousin in Clay County, Missouri, to another member of the family; the other is the outline of the movie script for *With a Song in My Heart*. The letter sheds light on one of the great mysteries of Jane's life, the disappearance of her father when she was five. The movie script is of particular value because Jane was the technical advisor on the film and helped to ensure that it portrayed her feelings and experiences accurately. By bringing these resources, other archival documents, and oral accounts of her later life together, I have been able to explore in detail the tragic, triumphant, and compelling life of Jane Froman.

Acknowledgments

The publication of this book ends a lengthy journey to correct an historical oversight—there is now a biography of Jane Froman. This happened because of the assistance, guidance, support, and advice I received from wonderful people that I met along the way.

Though she asked not to be thanked, it would be very wrong if I did not express my sincere appreciation to Becky Schroeder. From the moment we discussed my writing this book, I knew I had an unwavering advocate in the effort to preserve the memory of Jane Froman. Without her steady guidance and editorial skills, this book would never have happened.

Dr. Lawrence O. Christensen, professor emeritus at the University of Missouri–Rolla, was also of tremendous help. His attention to my manuscript and his insightful suggestions made it a much better document. I am thankful for the contribution of his thoughts and ideas.

One more person involved in the publication process deserves thanks: Gary Kass, my copyeditor at the University of Missouri Press. I learned a great deal from him and I appreciate all that he did.

I am also grateful to Columbia College, in particular to Dr. and Mrs. Gerald Brouder. When Dr. Brouder became president of the college in 1995, much of the Froman memorabilia was kept in a small and cluttered storeroom at the college. Under the supervision of the Brouders, especially Bonnie Brouder, this material is now properly housed and preserved so that scholars and other interested people can study and view it. Among the many papers that Bonnie "rescued" was Jane's unpublished autobiography. I am profoundly indebted to the Brouders and Columbia College for granting me permission to use that document as the basis for this book.

The Western Historical Manuscript Collection at the University of Missouri–Columbia has both the Jane Froman Papers and the Jane Froman Collection. It is a monumental accumulation of research material, and the people who work at the Collection made it easier for me to find my way through it. I thank them all for their help and professionalism. However, I would like to single out a few individuals whom I could always rely upon when I was in a quandary: Diane Ayotte, David Moore, William Stolz, and Sue McCubbin. I so appreciate their hard work.

From my very first visit to the Boone County Historical Society/Walters–Boone County Historical Museum, everyone was courteous and friendly. The current director, Deborah Thompson, and her staff have been nothing but helpful and considerate of whatever I needed. In addition, their annual Jane Froman Day celebration is a gift not only to the community of Columbia but also to all who cherish the Froman legacy.

The contributions made by the residents of Arrow Rock, Missouri, and the staff of the Henry County Historical Society, located in Clinton, Missouri, greatly added to this book.

There is yet another group of people whom I must thank. They are not scholars interested in learning all they can about Jane Froman. They do not have to do that. They already know about her because they were her friends. So many of these marvelous people shared their fond memories of Jane with me, helping me to better understand the type of person she was. I will never be able to properly thank them all— perhaps this book will do that. However, there are a few who deserve special mention: Robert and Dorothy Benson, Elizabeth Kennedy, Diane Dagley, Carol Peck, and Carol Kennedy. Each gave me something that Jane had—they gave me their friendship. It is a gift that is priceless and one that I will always cherish.

One person who did not know Jane but discovered her long after her career was over is Michael Modero. He is a collector of rare and quality Froman memorabilia, and has accumulated many important items. Over the years, Mike was always gracious whenever I had a question that needed an answer, and we have become good friends.

This book is the result of my efforts. If there are any omissions or misconceptions regarding Jane Froman, I am the one responsible—not the numerous people who assisted me. Since reading Jane's unpublished autobiography, I have wanted to let her "speak" about the events that shaped her life. I hope this book does not disappoint.

Jane Froman

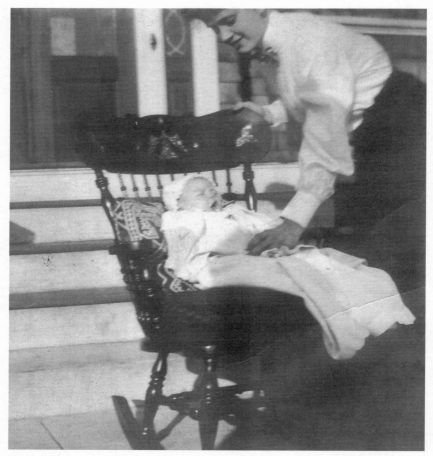

With her mother, Anna, looking on, an infant Jane enjoys the sunshine. (Western Historical Manuscript Collection, Columbia, Missouri)

1. *Anna and Elmer*

Billy Rose, the famous producer of musicals, was once asked to name the ten best female singers of the day. He replied, "There is Jane Froman and nine others."

Growing up in Henry and Boone counties in Missouri, Jane's thoughts about her future did not include becoming, in the opinion of many critics, the finest vocalist of her time. As she wrote in her unpublished autobiography: "My plans, if any, had been just like those of all the girls I knew—to marry and settle down in the good world of all our friends in Missouri where I was born, and to lead the rich full life of homemaking amongst them." Things did not work out as Jane intended. Instead, she wrote, she embarked upon a journey "which took me into that magic world of music and the theater and all over the globe." Her career also took her to the depths of despair and almost to her death.

Ellen Jane Froman was born in her parents' home at 26 Amherst Avenue in University City, a suburb of St. Louis, on Sunday, November 10, 1907. She weighed nine pounds and was named after her maternal grandmother, Ellender Jane Barcafer. Both Jane's father, Elmer Ellsworth Froman, and her mother, Anna Barcafer Froman, had a rich tradition of music in their family backgrounds. It would seem that Jane was destined to inherit great musical talent.

Her father was the fifth of six children born to William Gist Froman and Mary Sherard. All were sons. Born on June 29, 1868, in Plattsburg, Missouri, Elmer was named after a distant relative who had served as a Union soldier in the Civil War. William Froman subsequently divorced Mary and in June

1897 married Louisa Mae Higgins. He became the father of six more children—three girls and three boys. Because of Elmer's disappearance from her life, it is unlikely that Jane ever knew much of this second family or had any meaningful contact with her numerous Froman aunts, uncles, and cousins. As for Elmer, he grew into "a fine looking man, in fact, handsome, with a beautiful tenor voice," according to a cousin's letter.

Anna, born on January 15, 1874, in Clinton, Missouri, "came from a family of forceful, forthright people of high integrity and principle, all musical to their talented fingertips," Jane wrote. The Barcafer clan was a large one. "There were 13 brothers and sisters. . . . They all sang and played and performed in the family orchestra. . . . They were all proficient in music, both classical and current. . . . They sang in choirs and concerts, in schools, at socials . . . and were all vital members of the community."

The Barcafers were one of the prominent families of Clinton. Many residents of Henry County had strong pro-Southern sympathies during the Civil War, but Jane's grandfather, Thaddeus Barcafer, served in the Union Army, was wounded in the shoulder, and received a veteran's pension for his injury. Later, he became the probate judge of Henry County.

Jane particularly admired her Barcafer grandmother and aunts, whom she called "dauntless." She credited "their fighting spirits" with keeping her "alive for hours in those icy waters in February, 1943." She regarded her grandmother with wonder because of the way she managed all the activities of a large family. It made such an impression that decades later, Jane wrote in her autobiography:

I remember Grandma—she sang, of course—in all of her imposing stature and ceaseless activities. Grandma Barcafer, an amazing person in her own right, was a painter, and an artist, too, at homemaking for her great brood. In addition to the problems of her 13 children, she made and mended their clothes, churned the butter, tended the garden which supplied the family vegetables and fruit which she canned and preserved, ran the household with firm and knowledgeable hands and taught painting on the top floor of the old house. She made exquisite lace, much of which I still have. Those strong fingers were never idle. She also painted china with great delicacy and taste. . . . Every one of her children had an instrument and she was never too busy to listen to rehearsals of her family orchestra, or to correct any careless passages during rehearsal sessions in her living room.

While taking care of her large family and teaching art students, her grandmother still found the time to ship "her china paintings to 17 countries," according to an American Express order book Jane found years later.

One aunt that Jane learned to know well was her Aunt Pearl, "a remarkable character." Aunt Pearl sang in the church choir in York, Nebraska, for forty-five years and was also involved in community and social activities. She was known far and wide for her "many kindnesses and unfailing good sense." Through her lawyer husband, she came to know many prominent people of the day, including the great orator and presidential candidate William Jennings Bryan. Above all, however, when she was with Jane she gave her love and attention. And she shared something else with her niece that Jane felt was an invaluable gift: "It was Aunt Pearl who despite her crowded life taught me how to sew, to knit, to tat, to crochet. How often in my heart I have thanked her through the years. For without these skills so patiently and expertly passed on to me I would not have the use of my right hand and arm today." And so it went with all of Jane's Barcafer relatives: "They were all gifted. All well trained. And they loved their music. It was part and parcel of their lives, regardless of whatever field they eventually entered."

Jane's mother was the musical standout of the Barcafer clan. Anna began playing the piano at age five and earned money as an organist in a country church before graduating from Franklin High School in Clinton. She spent two years

Jane as a toddler, with perhaps a favorite toy. (Western Historical Manuscript Collection)

at Chicago Musical College studying piano, receiving her teacher's certificate in 1892, and stayed at the college another year for postgraduate study. She was an exceptional student, possessing "more than ordinary musical talent and

highly cultured both in vocal and instrumental music,"
according to a Clinton newspaper. For two consecutive years,
she received a diamond medal awarded for excellence in
classical music. While Anna was at Chicago Musical College,
according to Jane, Florenz Ziegfeld Jr., son of the president
of the college, squired her about town. Many years later,
Jane would star in a production of his famous Ziegfeld Follies.

After her studies in Chicago, Anna taught in Clinton and
St. Joseph, Missouri, where she sang in the church choir. It
was in St. Joseph that she met Jane's father, who also was a
member of the choir.

Elmer and Anna were married in Anna's hometown of
Clinton on March 7, 1898. The *Henry County Record* reported that on "Monday morning—at the residence of Mr. and
Mrs. Thad Barcafer, their daughter, Miss Anna Tillman, was
married to Elmer Ellsworth Froman of St. Joseph." The brief
article extols Anna's musical accomplishments and goes on
to say that "Mr. Froman is a well known young business man
of St. Joseph, holding a responsible position with the Hundley-
Frazier Dry Goods Co." In fact, the "responsible position"
Elmer held was that of a traveling salesman. A March 12 story
in the *Clinton Eye* detailed that after the wedding, Mr. and
Mrs. Elmer Froman "left on the afternoon Memphis train for
their future home in St. Joseph," then the third largest city
in Missouri.

During 1902 and 1903 Anna studied and performed in
Europe. Returning to Missouri, she opened a studio in St.
Louis and continued her singing and teaching. In 1904, at the
St. Louis World's Fair, Anna was the featured vocalist at many
state receptions including those for Kentucky, Maryland, and,
of course, Missouri. By then, according to the cousin's letter,
Elmer had a "position with a big mercantile firm, Rice, Stix &
Company at a salary of $300 and expenses," a substantial
yearly salary in those days. In 1907, when Jane was born in
her parents' University City home, her father still traveled,
selling his wares, and her mother gave music lessons.

A family portrait of Jane with her mother and grandmother. The identity of the man is unknown. It could be Jane's father, Elmer, or one of her Barcafer uncles. (Western Historical Manuscript Collection)

2. Jane and Margaret Ann

By the time Jane was five, Elmer had secured "a position with some big firm" in New York City, his cousin wrote. He traveled in the south "with a number of trunks, selling fine clothes, ball dresses, and such to rich people." It could not have been easy for Jane, having her father gone a good part of the time. But her life became even harder just prior to her fifth birthday. A clue to what happened can be found in Jane's baby book.

Attached to the back inside cover of the book is a very small newspaper obituary that states: "FROMAN—Entered into rest Tuesday, March 4, at 9:35 A.M. Margaret Ann Froman, infant daughter of Mr. and Mrs. Elmer Froman, at the age of 4 1/2 months." Nowhere in any other Froman material is there the slightest hint or clue that Jane had a sister. In fact, in numerous interviews that Jane gave throughout her career, she at times lamented the fact that she was an only child. She clearly wished that she had siblings but did not refer to a sister who had died in infancy. Most of Jane's friends say that she never said anything to them about a sister; some maintain there were rumors of a sister, but nothing for certain; and one acquaintance is sure that Jane told her she had a sister.

Was Margaret Ann older or younger than Jane? The obituary mentions that Margaret Ann "entered into rest Tuesday, March 4," although no year is given. A perpetual calendar unlocked the answer. Only two March 4 dates make any sense: Tuesday, March 4, 1902, and Tuesday, March 4, 1913. The March 4, 1902, date does not work because of Anna's European trip. That leaves March 4, 1913. This is the first concrete piece of information—it reveals that Jane, born November 10, 1907, had a younger sister.

With a death date for Margaret Ann, her date of birth can be calculated. Counting backwards four and a half months suggests that she was born in mid-October 1912, just a few weeks before Jane's fifth birthday. The Thursday, October 24, 1912, edition of the *Henry County Democrat* reported that "Mr. and Mrs. Frohman [the name was sometimes spelled with an *h*] of St. Louis are the proud parents of a little daughter born Monday night. Mrs. Frohman is formerly Anna Barcafer of Clinton." The birth certificate at the Missouri Department of Health states that Margaret Ann was born in St. Ann's Hospital in St. Louis on October 22, 1912, at 1 A.M. The document lists Elmer's age as forty-two and Anna's as thirty-eight. At the time, he was still a traveling salesman and she was a housewife.

Her death certificate reveals that Margaret Ann died in the same hospital in which she was born. She lived her brief life of four months and ten days in Ward 26, never having left the hospital. The cause of death was spina bifida and secondary meningitis. Spina bifida is a spinal defect in which some of the vertebrae fail to close during development, leaving part of the spinal cord uncovered. Today, doctors perform surgery in the womb to correct this condition, but in 1912 this was not possible. Margaret Ann was buried on March 5, 1913, the day after her death, at the Valhalla Cemetery in St. Louis.

The March 27, 1913, edition of the *Henry County Democrat* reported that "Mrs. E. E. Frohman and children arrived from St. Louis this morning for a visit with Mrs. E. J. Barcafer and family." This is curious, for no children could have arrived with Anna on March 27. Margaret Ann had died three weeks earlier and Jane was already in Clinton. According to Jane's autobiography, she had a throat infection when she was five and "the doctors advised that I be sent to my grandparents' house in Clinton to recuperate." Anna Froman must

Margaret Ann Froman's grave in the children's section of the Valhalla Cemetery in St. Louis, Missouri. (Photo by Jeff Stone)

have arrived in Clinton by herself. Perhaps there was more to the story than the public needed to know.

The hours that Anna and Elmer most likely spent with Margaret Ann, her doctors, and whatever medical specialists were available in 1912 would have left little time for Jane. However, being sent to her grandparents' house—either to recover from an illness or because there was a medical emergency in the family—is not a situation that would likely have had a profound effect on Jane. But she believed that something that happened in 1913 did, indeed, change her life. When Anna came back to Clinton, she came alone. Elmer was not with her, and this is the circumstance that Jane felt had such a devastating effect upon her.

I never saw my parents together again. And as time went on I began to realize that something I did not understand and which worried me was very much amiss between those people I loved so dearly. I had been very close to my father, and missed him terribly.

Mama came to live in Clinton, but Papa never did. At my questioning Mama made it very clear that Papa would not be joining us. She never talked of him again. Nor did I ever see him. What had occurred, why they parted, what caused the pain that separated these gifted young people remained locked in Mama's heart and she never revealed to the wondering daughter who loved him why Papa had gone another way. . . .

It was about this time that I heard someone say that I had a fabulous voice and I began to sing. Also I began to stutter. And it has plagued me all of my life.

It is puzzling that Jane does not refer to Margaret Ann in her autobiography—a document in which she was very open and honest about many things in her life. In her later years, she was a trailblazer in discussing painful topics of the day, including physical and mental disability issues, and she never hid her own medical problems from the public glare. It is hard to imagine why she would have been secretive about having a sister die at an early age of a terrible birth defect.

Perhaps the key to unlocking the mystery of Margaret Ann's effect on Jane lies in its connection to Jane's development and not with Jane's reluctance to openly and freely discuss the birth and death of her sister. As frightful as these events were, it is what resulted from them—the breakup of her parents' marriage—that was so painful to Jane. This would be an emotional trauma for any five-year-old. What was most important in Jane's life was that she had lost the father she deeply loved. At the same time, she also lost the ability to speak clearly and easily, or, as she once said, to "talk straight."

Researchers have made many attempts to determine the cause of stuttering, the inability to speak with ease that burdens some people. The perplexing thing about stuttering, in Jane's words, is its "maddening habit of coming and going." According to researchers, stutterers often are fluent when singing, as Jane was, and in certain speaking situations. At present, there is no consensus on what causes people to stutter, although there are many theories. Physiological reasons, learned behavior origins, and psychological causes have all been put forward as possible culprits for the problem. An analysis of research in the field by Tracie Randolph, included on the web page of the University of Minnesota–Duluth, discussed these various opinions.

Some experts believe there are physiological reasons that connect stuttering to genetic factors—stuttering may run in families. Then there are researchers convinced that stuttering is a learned behavior in which a person is conditioned to speak disfluently. Others point to psychological causes, claiming that those who stutter are "trying to cope, unconsciously, with [a] repressed need," such as "a person who feels hostility toward someone and does not express this anger openly."

Jane's stuttering appears to fall into the third theory relating to the cause of stuttering. Her parents' marriage was torn apart, and she never again saw the father she adored. She had much to be angry about. No matter the theory, the fact remains that at age five Jane experienced a traumatic emotional event that she believed affected her for the rest of her life.

As to what happened to Elmer, no conclusive answer has been found. A clue appears in the 1950 letter from one Froman cousin to another:

He was in Atlanta, where he was staying in a hotel. The story was that he came down out of his room one night, bareheaded, and asked for a certain kind of cigar and a New York newspaper. He was told that he could get these things two blocks down the street, but that they did not have these things at the hotel. He went out bareheaded, and started down the street, and that was the last that was seen of him.

The letter goes on to say that after Elmer's disappearance "the hotel people, the firm he worked for in New York, and Elmer Froman's wife began to try to find out what had become of him," but to no avail; he had vanished without a trace; to this day, no one seems to know precisely what happened to him or why he disappeared. There are many questions, but no answers. Did he meet with some kind of injury? Was he running away from what he considered to be an intolerable situation regarding his infant daughter, Margaret Ann? Or did he decide to leave his family for some other reason?

Through the years, there were Elmer "sightings" in various parts of the country. According to the cousin's letter, "one woman said that she had later seen Elmer in a big hotel in San Francisco." The cousin speculates that Elmer obtained a divorce from Anna in Pennsylvania, then remarried and settled in Ohio. But at best, this is all supposition. The only thing that is certain is that Elmer was gone. From the day he left in 1912, Jane never saw or heard from him again.

3. Clinton and the Convent

With her husband gone and her second child deceased, Jane's mother returned to her hometown of Clinton, Missouri, to start her life over again. It would not be easy. She was now a single parent, a daunting situation today but even more so then. However, she would not be alone. She moved into her parents' home at 214 East Jefferson, a huge house with a long tradition of sheltering a large family.

As was natural, Anna turned to music to support herself and her daughter. In addition, she had debts to pay, some presumably related to the expenses of providing for Margaret Ann's care, her death, and her burial. So Anna gave music lessons, vocal as well as piano, for a dollar an hour.

About this time, Jane's musical abilities became apparent. At bedtime, she and her mother would sing together. Her famed musical ear was evident early. At age five, she heard the music of a carousel at a carnival and later played the tunes on the piano. She only had to hear melodies once and then could play them perfectly. Around the time she was eight years old, Jane was singing at local churches and parties.

On September 1, 1913, Ellen Jane Froman started school at the Holy Rosary Academy in Clinton. It was a new phase in her childhood. The academy, established the year before by Father Edward Fitzgerald, was an elementary and high school staffed by the Sisters of St. Joseph of Concordia. While the nuns administered the academy, it was not a parochial school but a private boarding facility for girls. The teachers did not receive a salary; they were supposed to subsist on the fees paid by boarding students. However, the academy

This rare photo of Jane when she was a schoolgirl in Clinton, perhaps at the age of five or six, was found in her baby book. (Columbia College)

attracted only one boarder in its first year instead of the thirty or so expected, and something had to be done to change this situation.

The nuns initiated a fund-raising campaign that included entertainment and dramatic programs performed by the day students. The upper floor of the academy was transformed into a theater, complete with stage, lights, and seats. Shows were given during holidays such as Thanksgiving and Christmas, and additional recitals were presented as well. The hard work and efforts of the students and staff were rewarding. Not only did the day students enjoy putting on the shows, but their parents also appreciated the artistic education they received. Boarding enrollment increased; even though most students were non-Catholic, the school flourished until 1924, when it was forced to close its doors, according to church history, because of a surge of intolerance that swept through that part of Missouri.

Jane attended the academy as a day student. But whenever Anna's music teaching took her away from Clinton, Jane lived at the academy with the nuns and the other boarding students. On every occasion that her mother left town, Jane was apprehensive. "I recall in those early years singing for some convent visitors . . . in French . . . with tears streaming down my cheeks. Mama had just left." She could "hear the chugging of the train growing fainter and fainter, leaving me a very lonely and frightened little girl. It was my darkest hour."

These were hard days for Jane, but in many ways they taught her how to endure terrible times and gave her the fortitude she would need later in life.

We were poor indeed in those days. In the cruel unheeding manner of children who have everything my classmates made me feel I was not one of them. The clothes I wore were not like theirs. I couldn't recite the poetry lesson. I didn't have a father. I couldn't recite the poetry lesson because the words simply would not come out. I stuttered so badly that the children laughed and joked among themselves. The nuns seeing my predicament soon ceased to call on me for recitations. I knew that horror known to the little child who's made to feel she's "different." I was apart. I took refuge in my singing where stuttering never interfered. It was the only way I knew how to communicate.

While at the academy, Jane came to feel that the circumstances of her life were "broken." She was constantly being reminded of the "contrast of home and belonging to [a] 'good family' with the attendant social life on one hand and [the] chill, lonely atmosphere of [the] convent on the other." She seemed always mindful of the stigma of coming from a broken home and the fact that she had a working mother. The memories of these early hardships stayed with Jane all of her life, contributing to her empathy for others as she grew older.

Her feelings of loneliness, of being an outsider, of being ridiculed, added to Jane's strong stubborn streak. On one occasion, she expressed her displeasure at the poor quality of food the boarding students received—she went "down to the dining room at night and poured grapenuts all over the floor." One can only imagine the havoc that this caused for the nuns in the morning.

There were other moments of rebellion. With a child's fascination and curiosity to see something that she was not supposed to witness, Jane peeked "through [a] transom at night to watch nuns shave [their] heads." At the convent she received her "first whipping" for visiting the home of a friend whose mother was considered "fast" by the standards of the day. And there was more defiance to come.

It was no surprise that Jane was "the prize musical student at the convent" and that the nuns often asked her to perform for visitors so that they could marvel at her voice. But her gift for music also got Jane into trouble. "It came very easily for me," Jane wrote, "to play everything I heard by ear. Once I got to the convent, however, natural aptitude did not suffice and hours of practice were inevitable." Stubborn and proud of her ability, Jane balked—"who practices when you

Jane's musical talents were nurtured at an early age. This photo shows her posing in a dance costume. (Western Historical Manuscript Collection)

could play everything anyway." She retaliated by biting "the piano from one end of the music stand to the other, fiercely and destructively." Her teeth marks were everywhere. The mother superior reported to Anna that "Ellen Jane has bitten the piano," and Anna paid to have the piano restored. The determination that Jane displayed as a child was sometimes subdued, but it was never conquered. It would reappear from time to time as she got older, and it was a quality that served her well after 1943.

Though Jane won all the musical honors the academy had to offer, she did not fare as well in other subjects. Eventually, her years in Clinton and her schooling at the convent came to an end. Her grade school days were over, and once again it was time to move. This time it would be to Columbia, Missouri, a college town located in the heart of the state, about 120 miles from both St. Louis to the east and Kansas City to the west. There Jane would attend high school and college and find the place that, as the years passed and her love for it grew, she came to call home.

4. Columbia and College

When Anna would travel from Clinton, leaving Jane at the academy, it was not only to give music lessons. She also was the choir leader for the Reverend Arthur Neal Lindsey, the minister of the Christian Church in Clinton. A renowned clergyman, Lindsey "conducted many big revival meetings in different parts of the South and [Anna] was the song leader for Dr. Lindsey in some of these revivals, maybe most of them."

In addition to his religious pursuits, Lindsey also engaged in political activities. In 1917, he sought the Democratic nomination for governor. He was unsuccessful, but remained active in the Missouri Democratic Party and later served as a Missouri state senator from 1934 to 1938. With his background and the connections that came with it, Lindsey was able to help secure for Anna the position of director of voice at Christian College in 1920.

Christian College (now called Columbia College) was one of the more prestigious girls' schools in Missouri. Jane remembered it as "the best girls' school for young ladies in our part of the world. . . . It was fine scholastically and small. It was exclusive. It was particular about the girls accepted. It was topnotch. It was just the place, Mama believed, for her daughter, Ellen Jane, to go to school."

Anna taught music while Jane went to classes. They lived on the campus of the college, which at the time offered both a high school diploma and a two-year college degree. The year that Jane enrolled, the college installed a new president, Edgar D. Lee. He believed in promoting student participation in campus activities, and the students at Christian were

The swimming pool at Christian College. Note the height of the rafters from which, friends said, Jane dived into the water. (Columbia College)

encouraged to keep busy. Jane sang in school productions, at churches, and in local benefit shows. Also, she and her mother often "sang together at the musicales in the private homes of people who in those days loved to entertain their friends in that way." For Jane, there were drawbacks to being a student at Christian. She found it "rather irksome being [the] daughter of [a] faculty member. Any infraction of [the] rules [would] be severely punished."

Jane's curious, adventuresome, and stubborn personality was hard to keep in check. On one occasion, while swimming in the college pool, she decided to show off. School legend has it that she climbed onto the rafters—a height of about twelve feet—and dived into the pool. To Sue Gerard, a Columbia writer who taught at the college for many years, the idea of the five-foot, six-inch Jane "plunging through the air headfirst and arching back up in seven feet, two inches [of water] sounds impossible." She believes that Jane must have jumped feet first. But however she did it, Jane caused quite a commotion, and the legend persists.

Like most high school students, Jane looked forward to summer vacation and time away from books, teachers, and the classroom. When she was fifteen, however, she had to spend part of her summer in school to supplement her regular course work. She enrolled at Central Methodist College in Fayette, a small town some twenty miles outside Columbia. She boarded there for the summer session and registered for two classes—American literature and physiology, narrowly passing both. Academics were just not for her.

More often, Anna and Jane spent summers at Schroon Lake in the Adirondack Mountains of New York. Oscar Seagle, a famed concert baritone and voice teacher, had established a music camp nearby that attracted outstanding and experienced performers along with others who were interested in studying all aspects of music. It was a place where the campers would not be disturbed by outside distractions. Both mother and daughter enjoyed the surroundings, and years later Jane would try to recreate such a camp in Arrow Rock, Missouri.

Jane earned her high school diploma at Christian College and stayed for two more years to obtain her associate of arts degree in 1926. This allowed her to teach in the public schools of Missouri. But Jane wanted something else. So, after graduating from Christian, she enrolled in the University of Missouri in Columbia. Her mother was undoubtedly proud of her. Anna, as a "respected and honored member of the [Christian College] faculty, . . . was admired by everyone," and Jane was her "well-brought-up daughter." It was expected that Jane would continue to be her mother's child, a model daughter. However, Jane was her own person—independent and with a mind of her own. Her dreams eventually clashed with Anna's expectations for her.

Anna Froman-Hetzler in 1929, the year she retired as director of voice at Christian College. In 1920, she organized a singing ensemble there called the Christian College Sextet. Today, that group is called the Jane Froman Singers. (Christian College Yearbook, *June 1929. State Historical Society of Missouri, Columbia)*

Photograph of Jane taken in 1926 when she graduated from Christian College. (Western Historical Manuscript Collection)

Once Jane entered the University of Missouri, she quickly became part of the college social scene and "had a ball." There was never a party to which she was invited that she declined to attend. Jane was once asked if she "had any idea how many hundreds of miles I had danced at the fraternity parties while attending the University of Missouri!" She wrote:

I remember only that if it became a choice between a dance and a school book, I was at the dance. I was elected to Kappa Kappa Gamma, one of the leading social sororities on the campus. I was pinned, of course, and sometimes I had as many as five pins tucked away somewhere out of sight—one was supposed to be the limit. They like to tell me here in Missouri that church services never were so crowded with eligible young men as when I sang the solos at First Christian Church, which was frequently. Anyway that's the legend about town and I like to believe it. Life was all grand and gay and wonderful.

Jane loved a good party, a good time, as she always would. But in addition to her social activities, she had her sights set on something else—getting into a yearly musical revue.

When Jane entered the university, she chose journalism as her major. This might seem a strange choice for her to make, considering her stutter. What is even more unusual is that she declared she wanted to be an interviewer. But, as she wrote in her autobiography, she was doing precisely what she wanted to do, and journalism was actually the furthest thing from her mind. "I had entered the School of Journalism, though no one else was aware of it, with one sole purpose in mind. I wanted to be in the annual musical comedy given by the School of Journalism. This I attained."

After she enrolled at the university, she was out from under Anna's constant influence; the constraints of being the daughter of a college faculty member were gone, and so was the pressure of having to live up to expectations that were not hers. Jane felt free to do whatever she desired. Knowing exactly what she wanted, she went after it and succeeded.

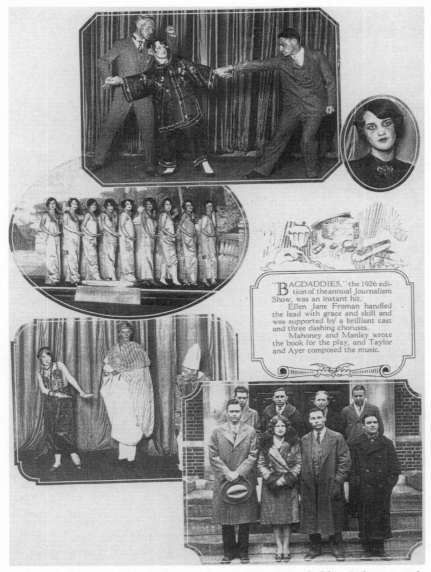

"BAGDADDIES," the 1926 edition of the annual Journalism Show, was an instant hit.

Ellen Jane Froman handled the lead with grace and skill and was supported by a brilliant cast and three dashing choruses.

Mahoney and Manley wrote the book for the play, and Taylor and Ayer composed the music.

Scenes from Jane's first starring performance, in "Bagdaddies," the musical presented by the University of Missouri School of Journalism in December 1926. (The Savitar, 1927. University of Missouri Archives, Columbia)

She was not only in the journalism musical show, but she accomplished much more.

I had become the lead in this class musical, "Bagdaddies," written by students at the school, Elmer Taylor and Frederick W. Ayer. I had danced and sung, "Mystic Moon," the hit number of the show. As a result, a Skouras representative in the audience engaged me for a week in St. Louis for the children's annual Christmas show at the Grand Central Theater. A pretty little girl called Betty Grable shared the dressing room with me. We talked about it many years after when we were in Hollywood.

This was Jane's first taste of show business. She was billed as "Ellen Jane Froman, the 'Blues Singing Co-ed of Missouri University.' . . . I was paid $100 for the week—$75 of which I blew on a fancy beaded dress, high fashion in the roaring 20s." The *Columbia Missourian* gave Jane front-page coverage for her role in "Bagdaddies" and again for her performance in St. Louis. It was just the beginning of the publicity she was to receive.

This success and attending all those college parties came with a price—it took a toll on her studies. Seemingly before she knew it, Jane suddenly "flunked out" of the University of Missouri and its school of journalism. To Anna, this was a disgrace beyond understanding, an embarrassment that she could not tolerate.

As Jane wrote, "Her shame for me and herself was great." Anna believed that "people did what they set out to do. She had done it herself, and she expected her daughter Ellen Jane to do the same." Jane contended that she had actually done exactly what Anna had taught her. "As a matter of fact, I had indeed accomplished what I set out to do." She not only got a part in the musical, but she was the star. This did not matter to Anna—it was not what she wanted for Jane. "The attainment of my secret ambition did not alter the public disgrace in Mama's eyes. Daughter Ellen Jane despite all of her mother's efforts had failed, not only in her eyes but also in the eyes of the faculty and people of the town. Something had to be done about it. Ellen Jane had to be put in harness."

Unwittingly, Anna initiated two events that put Jane on the path that would lead to show business stardom. The first followed from her displeasure with Jane for not doing well at the university. "To Mama it was such a disgrace that she made arrangements forthwith to get me out of town as quickly as possible—I was dispatched to Cincinnati." In the fall of 1928, Anna saw to it that her daughter enrolled in the Cincinnati Conservatory of Music, where she "lived at the Conservatory and threw myself into the music life of the school." The second event occurred shortly after Jane's arrival at the conservatory. "I did not realize how completely on my own I was to be until the dean of women called me into her office one fine day and told me that Mama had married again."

Anna's new husband belonged to a prominent Columbia family. "She had married the mayor of our town, William J. Hetzler, was retiring from teaching, and now had a fine and imposing home of her own. She had become the first lady of Columbia. Henceforth, hers was to be a new and busy life, apart from mine." Why Jane felt she could no longer depend on her mother, why Anna's new life made her feel "apart" from her, is not explained in Jane's autobiography. For whatever reason, Jane wrote, "I realized all too clearly that Mama no longer belonged to me alone and since she had another life to lead I could not continue to be her responsibility. Something had to be done about it, and I did it."

Anna's sending Jane away to the Cincinnati Conservatory and her remarriage were turning points in Jane's life. Jane felt she was now on her own, dependent on no one but herself. She had to survive and make her own way in the world. To do this, Jane turned to the one thing she had that everyone wanted—they wanted to hear her sing. She began to purposefully use her musical talent, and a show business career was not far behind.

5. Radio and Vaudeville

Determined now to pay her own way at the Cincinnati Conservatory of Music, Jane found ways to support herself. She discovered, by accident, that the conservatory provided a scholarship of three hundred dollars. That sum would go a long way toward helping her meet her expenses. However, only girls from the senior class were eligible for the award and she was a freshman. But Jane rarely took "no" for an answer, and she did not do so this time: "My mind worked quickly. I had to have that scholarship."

When the auditions for the scholarship were held in the conservatory's auditorium, Jane showed up with her music.

I begged [the judges] to be heard, but was refused. I insisted. They demurred. I kept on insisting. More to humor and get rid of me than anything else, they gave in and I sang my first song. There was silence. Then I was asked to sing again, and then again. I won the scholarship, and with it enough money to get by on.

As generous as the scholarship was, Jane felt she needed still more financial aid. She went to the president of the conservatory and asked if she could find her outside work—"work for pay." The president agreed to help, and before long Jane was "booked at parties, teas and soirees. I sang classics, ballads, operatic arias and pops, and I played my own accompaniments to them all." One tea was in honor of the wife of Ohio's senator, Robert A. Taft. Jane was paid ten dollars for her performance.

The professional musical career of Jane Froman had begun

and, to no one's surprise, Jane was a success wherever she sang. She was in demand and she "loved every bit" of this life. Twenty-one and full of "spirit and vitality," she "loved the pretty clothes and dressing up in them." In addition to performing at private functions, she sang in the church choir and earned ten dollars each Sunday.

Vivacious and friendly, Jane acquired many friends and attended many parties. One evening, she was a guest at a social gathering at the home of a friend. During the party, Jane was asked to play the piano and sing, and "for an hour and a half I sang songs old and new, popular and classical." One of the guests was Powel Crosley Jr., owner of the Cincinnati Reds baseball team and of WLW, "the largest independent radio station in the country." He asked Jane if she had ever thought of singing on the radio and offered her an audition at his station for the following morning. By the next evening, Jane was on the radio.

At first she did commercials for Tom's Toasted Peanuts at ten dollars a program and sang for as many as twenty-two shows a week, including "one at 5 A.M. for the farmers." Because she was working so many hours, the station asked her to become a "permanent staff artist" at eighty-five dollars a week. "Well, it meant security and of course I took it."

Life in Cincinnati was good. I had friends. There were parties and much gaiety as well as my work, which kept me busy. My life was varied and active. I knew everyone in town and they all knew me and invited me everywhere. I was very sensitive about my stuttering, but strangely enough no one else seemed to care.

Jane remained at WLW for two years. While she was there, she learned all she could about the world of show business and she was "fascinated by it all." At the same time, people were learning about her. One of those people was the celebrated orchestra leader Paul Whiteman, known as the "King of Jazz."

Whiteman sent Jane a telegram saying that he was going to be appearing in Cincinnati with his band and wanted to meet with her, but WLW did not want its top performer lured away. Saying that Jane needed to rest a sore throat, the station management sent her away on a two-week, all-expenses-paid vacation. It just happened to be the same two weeks that Whiteman was in Cincinnati. Jane wrote that when she returned, "Paul Whiteman and his company had left town and I continued with my programs and my social life in Cincinnati."

While at WLW, Jane met a performer named Donald McKaig Ross, part of the vaudeville team of Brooks and Ross, who felt that after two years in Cincinnati it was time for Jane to go on to bigger things. He believed she had the "makings of a star" but that she would never become one unless she moved on. In 1931, he convinced Jane to accompany Brooks and Ross to Chicago to see what the Windy City had to offer.

Jane arrived in Chicago with no job and only two hundred dollars to her name. Though she had a bright future ahead of her, it did not seem that way at first. Along with Brooks and Ross, she auditioned for CBS Radio. Brooks and Ross were offered a contract immediately, but Jane heard the network's musical director remark: "The team is fine. But I wouldn't give that girl $25 a week," a statement he probably came to regret. Jane was "crushed," and Don Ross was "infuriated. He knew a star when he saw one, and in his mind I was already a star," Jane wrote in her autobiography. "With indignation he went over to the other great radio station of the town, NBC, and made an appointment for an audition" for her.

In her haste, as she was leaving her hotel to go to the NBC audition, Jane caught her right heel and fell down a flight of stairs. Her right ankle was broken. Many people in her situation might have called the radio station and asked for a postponement. Not Jane. She did not want to miss the audition and the opportunity it might bring. Displaying the physical toughness and strength of character that would become her hallmark, she kept the appointment.

Jane was a big personality in the early days of radio. (Western Historical Manuscript Collection)

It never occurred to me to ask for a postponement. I was carried to the studio. I sang song after song for the musical director with my leg propped up and the mike on a table. At the end of the session I was told I had a job, and promptly fainted dead away from pain. But not before the musical director had congratulated me and I heard him say, "I've been trying to get hold of you for a long time." His name was Paul Whiteman.

Jane's radio career soon soared. NBC put her under contract with the network. She was paid $125 a week to appear on *Florsheim Frolics,* a show sponsored by the Florsheim Shoe Company. Whiteman offered Jane her own orchestra and a fifteen-minute show five evenings a week. Airing at 6:15, immediately after the popular *Amos 'n' Andy,* Jane's show was broadcast to all NBC radio stations across the country. In addition, Jane performed on other shows as well. She recalled that all of this was "great exposure."

I simply couldn't be missed wherever there was a radio set. And radio sets had sprung up like mushrooms all over the country. . . . My life in public had now begun for sure—publicity, promotion, photographers, interviews, public appearances, here there and everywhere. I was no longer the "blues singing co-ed of Missouri." I was "Radio Melody Queen," "Radio's Loveliest Songbird," and "Radio's Sweetest Songbird." Make your own choice. They certainly did in those days. I was developing my own style of singing a song and bringing to it every bit of musical knowledge I had acquired. . . . And I couldn't help but be aware of the fact that I was on my way.

Jane was indeed on her way and ready to make choices about her career. Whiteman wanted her to go on tour with him and his orchestra, but she feared that if she became known as a band singer, her career would not progress as rapidly as it otherwise might. So, after only six months, she ended her contract with Whiteman. They parted amicably, and she received a new contract from NBC.

Her work on radio brought her to the attention of people

in another form of entertainment—musical theater. Jane first saw her "name in lights" and had her "first great failure" at the same time when she was asked to perform at the "hottest theater in town"—Chicago's Oriental Theater. After just a few years of radio work, Jane was now going to vaudeville, a still-popular theatrical genre that included all types of performers: dancers, comedians, actors doing short plays, acrobats, animal acts, and, of course, singers like Jane.

In Chicago it was considered a great coup to appear there [the Oriental Theater] at the four-a-day performances. After weeks of negotiations in which I had been offered an original $250, I had settled for $1000 for a week's engagement, plus star billing. I appeared on the bill with the matchless Mills Brothers, who, as always, were a smash. My routine consisted entirely of songs listed as "most popular" in Variety, the bible of show business.

The response to Jane's performance was "sensational!" She and the Mills Brothers, a singing quartet, were asked to stay over for another week. For the second week, however, against all advice, Jane changed her musical routine.

I went back to the classics for my songs, none of which was on the "most popular" list. I was definitely not a smash! I was a complete and utter flop. You could hear the waves of boredom thundering down the aisles. I barely got to the wings. What a lesson! It was the same theater, the same singer, the gown was right, the singing was right, but the songs were dead wrong. They were not the songs the people in this Oriental audience were in the mood to hear. They wanted to hear music of their own day, not the music of the past. And I learned a lesson. I learned that an audience won't be forced.

After that first disastrous performance, Jane returned to singing what the audience wanted to hear, and once again, she was "a smash" and became "Jane Froman, a recognized singer in the new and exciting world of music." Giving audiences what they wanted was something Jane did for the rest of her career. She brought her beautiful contralto voice to all the popular songs of the day. According to many reviewers, no one sang a song with more clarity, passion, and sentiment, be it classical or popular, than Jane Froman. Throughout her career, audiences, critics, and fans loved the Froman style.

It was costly being "Jane Froman." While never "extravagant in my personal wardrobe," Jane did believe that "for the stage and for my acts . . . luxury, perhaps even extravagance must be the rule." There were costs for gowns, jewelry, musical arrangements, travel, hotels, restaurants, and more. The magnificent salary she received allowed Jane to maintain the appearance necessary for a successful entertainer.

While in Chicago, Jane lived close to the NBC studio in a one-room apartment. Despite her heavy schedule and all it entailed, she did enjoy some leisure activity. She was a passionate golfer, and "did manage somehow to swing a brassy" as well as to "get to the [Chicago Cubs] baseball games." All her life, Jane was an enthusiastic sports fan, "even though as life went on I couldn't take part in them myself anymore."

As Jane's popularity grew, she was often asked to travel to New York to make guest appearances on the top-rated radio shows that originated from there. Her most vivid first memory of New York, however, had nothing to do with her performances or the city's bright lights or fabulous nightlife. Instead, it concerned a new way to cope with an old nemesis.

My most pleasant moment in the big town as I now recall it was the discovery of all those little buttons at my bedside in the St. Regis Hotel. When I needed something, a gown pressed in a hurry, service in my room, the papers, I merely pressed a button. I didn't have to force myself to talk into the telephone. My stuttering continued to bother me.

Jane's anxiety about her stuttering persisted, yet it never deterred her from advancing her singing career. When she had been in Chicago for two years, she felt ready to make another move. The time had come to take on bigger things, to no longer make the occasional trip to New York for guest appearances, but rather to move there permanently. Don Ross, having left his vaudeville partner, had already gone. New York was where careers were made; it was "the big time," and Jane's goal became to make it there.

Don Ross, Jane's first husband, introduced her to the world of show business.
(Western Historical Manuscript Collection)

6. New York and Fame

Jane arrived in New York in January 1933, hoping for success, fame, and fortune. She was to achieve it all. But in that cold winter, as she embarked on a new chapter in her career, all she knew was that she had a hundred dollars in her pocket and, like most Americans during the Great Depression, needed work.

Jane was not unknown in the booming world of radio when she moved to New York, but she had yet to hit it big. Don Ross, whom she would marry in September, heard of an opening on one of the nation's most popular radio shows, *The Chesterfield Hour,* and he arranged for her to have an audition. She got the job and became part of an entertainment lineup that boasted some of the leading singers of the day, including Bing Crosby. All of this had happened within one week of her arrival in New York. Before long, Jane was known as "the Chesterfield Lark." Her career had taken a giant leap forward, and she was to stay with *The Chesterfield Hour* for years. Jane was thrilled. Don was pleased. However, not everyone Jane cared about was happy for her.

Mama's friends in Missouri tell me that they will never forget the look on her face when the voice of the "Lark" first wafted into Mama's sitting room—the voice she had loved and trained in all the enduring beauty of the classics, singing the blues, torch songs and ballads in such vivid contrast to the strains of Mama's own musical heritage. . . . She evidently took it in her stride though she never really approved, I'm sure, of the songs she heard me singing on the air. Mama, who . . . had devoted her life to the great classical composers, really looked

down her nose at what was going on in the music of the day which she
never really liked or understood.

Jane had different ideas: "I, on the contrary, had a great
and genuine feeling for those ballads and blues and torch
songs then coming into vogue. I very deliberately tried to
bring to these 'pops' not only the feeling and heart of the songs
but the musical taste and knowledge of phrasing and diction
I had acquired through the years."

Jane's intuitions and musical savvy served her well. "It
was my pride and joy as time went on to be able to bring my
musical know-how to the unforgettable songs of Gershwin,
Cole Porter, Dick Rodgers, Irving Berlin, Hoagy Carmichael
and oh so many who had been contributing to the great resur-
gence of American music."

If the world of music was changing, so was Jane's life. She
was on *The Chesterfield Hour* every Tuesday and Friday, and
those appearances "literally catapulted me into the big time."
With success came demands that were not always so welcome.

As my salary went up and up and up, so did my responsibilities. . . .
[Singing] took everything I had. It was no longer just pure fun for the
fun of singing. You disciplined yourself for every waking hour. You
didn't drink, you didn't stay up late at night—I never had anyway. But
you guarded almost fanatically your voice, your time and every bit of
your resources, physical and vocal. You were there in that vast studio
whenever they wanted you, and they wanted you all the time—morning, noon and night. I was no longer alone in a heavily draped room
with a tiny mike, but in the huge new studios with their large and
critical audiences. . . . By now that innocent looking little mike had
become a master. It certainly had become mine.

Despite the downside, Jane enjoyed her newfound fame.
She had more requests to sing than she could possibly accept.
Some of those offers came from movie theaters, which in
those days provided live entertainment in addition to show-
ing films. Jane appeared at such movie palaces as the famed

Radio City Music Hall, which she, being a perfectionist, considered too large for a singer to be able to perform in flawlessly. New York's Paramount Theater, though, was one place that she felt was first-rate for a singer, and she was very successful when she appeared there, which was often.

Things were going well for Jane, but they got even better when she was asked to become a cast member of the Ziegfeld Follies. The Follies had been introduced by theatrical producer Florenz Ziegfeld Jr. in 1907. His annual shows were lavish musical productions that featured beautiful women, comedy routines, elaborate costumes, and spectacular scenery. Although Ziegfeld had died the year before, there was to be a new edition of the Follies in 1933 and the producers wanted Jane to be part of it.

She would be joining a group of performers that included dancer Buddy Ebsen, comedian Fred Allen, actor Bob Cummings (who was from Joplin, Missouri), and the incomparable Fanny Brice, world-renowned actor, comedian, and singer. It was the beginning of a long and loyal friendship between Jane and Fanny. The new Follies went to Boston for a trial engagement, as most shows did before opening on Broadway. Due to her radio commitments, Jane commuted between Boston and New York. It was a heavy schedule but she managed it. However, never having been in a production as elaborate as the Follies, Jane was "terrified." Fanny Brice came to her rescue.

It was Fannie Brice who molded my first awkward movements on the stage. . . .

We became friends. From then on she took me in tow. She began to show me the ropes—how to walk across the stage, how to carry myself, head erect and body straight, and how to use my hands— above all how to use my hands.

She watched me, she corrected me and she made me practice over and over again all during the performances on the road, passing on to me [who was] just starting out in the field, her own great fund of priceless experiences.

Jane never forgot the kindness that Fanny showed to her and, long after the Follies ended, Fanny still had a soft spot for Jane. She always seemed to be there when Jane needed an extra boost of support.

Dear Fanny! Years later after the war, Hollywood was agog when she made one of her rare appearances as, still limping badly and with steel braces, I opened at the Mocambo. Fanny, who never went anywhere at night and never went to night clubs, had recognized my plight as she had so many years before and was there to spur me on once more.

Finally, the time came to move the production to New York. During Christmas week of 1933, the show opened at the Winter Garden Theater. The anticipation among the cast members was high. Jane wrote that after the run in Boston, they were "letter-perfect," but as the New York theater critics and the discriminating New York theatergoers began to arrive, their anxiety level rose. There was no need to worry—the show was a "smash" and Jane was "a star in the show." She sang several songs, but two stood out. One was "The House Is Haunted," which Billy Rose, who was Fanny Brice's husband at the time, wrote for her. The other was "What Is There to Say," which became a standard for her.

In spite of all the publicity and fame, Jane and Don tried to live quietly. They were able to put some money aside, and soon purchased a penthouse on East Seventy-ninth Street. Their new home had a terrace where Jane "managed to grow tomatoes . . . from two ponderous plants carefully brought from Missouri." Though a Missouri girl at heart, Jane did love the glitz and glamour of the show business world.

With it all of course came the excitement of sequin gowns . . . furs and posh restaurants, and the Rolls Royce, and that great intriguing, fascinating sparkle of the theater world. I gloried in it and I came in contact with all the big performers and artists of the day.

Jane remained with the Follies for a year. During this time,

Being part of the Ziegfeld Follies was an important step for Jane both professionally and personally. She recalled that her career "zoomed" and she made a lifelong friend in Fanny Brice. (From the collection of Ilene Stone)

she was in continuous demand. Her radio schedule was grueling, as was her recording schedule. It seemed that she was on every popular, top-rated show that was broadcast. In 1934, she was a weekly regular on no less than seven radio shows. Her name began to appear at the top of popularity polls. "Newspapers, magazines, trade papers, every town and hamlet seemed to have them, in great voting contests to determine who were the favorites on the air." Jane competed with such popular personalities as Jack Benny, George Burns and Gracie Allen, Bing Crosby and Guy Lombardo. The press referred to her by many names: "The sapphire song bird, or the blues singer with the Belasco touch [David Belasco was an American theatrical producer] . . . and even as [the] orchid lined voice!" All of this resulted in Jane being named the number-one female singer on the air in 1934. She had "reached the ephemeral pinnacle known as 'Success' with a capital S."

Stealing moments away for some relaxation was something that Jane always tried to do. She and Don took a car trip west to visit family and friends. Loving golf, Jane got out to the course as often as she could to "swing a club." And "every once in a while I flew back to Missouri to the home of Mayor and Mrs. Hetzler to see the Missouri Tigers play a football game."

Sometimes Mrs. Hetzler came to visit Jane and Don in New York. The Rosses "would knock ourselves out. We would get her tickets for concerts, for theaters and museums." Anna enjoyed "meeting all of the stars, even though she didn't thoroughly approve of them musically." During one visit, Jane gave a big party in Anna's honor, and she hobnobbed with New York's entertainment elite, enjoying herself immensely.

Though Jane was able to periodically flee her arduous performing schedule, there was something she could not escape from—her stuttering. She was forever fearful that when she was on the radio and had to talk instead of sing, she would not be able to speak easily and fluently. "I could never be

When Jane and Don traveled to Columbia to visit with Anna, this was the home they came to—the mayor's house at One West Broadway. It was the home of Anna's new husband, William J. Hetzler. (Western Historical Manuscript Collection)

confident of speaking words into the mike." To handle this situation, and avoid potential embarrassment, the radio shows always had someone speak for Jane. On many shows, Jane's radio "voice" was Arlene Francis, who later had a successful career in television. Off the air, Jane never hid her speech problem; in fact, there were numerous newspaper and magazine stories about her speaking difficulties.

However, there was one memorable time, during the radio show *Stage Door Canteen,* when she did talk for herself. On that occasion, the performer who was to read Jane's words dropped the script. "In the panic of the moment the words came rushing to my lips and I delivered them letter perfect to the astonishment of everyone, myself included." This was not the norm. It was not until many years later that Jane would no longer require another "voice" to speak for her when she performed. She would eventually learn how to speak for herself, but then, in those heady days of new success, fame, and triumph, she never again spoke while she was on the air.

But Jane continued to sing with a perfection with which she could not speak. Even busy presidents learned to know and value the beauty and uniqueness of the Froman voice. "Several times I was summoned to sing at the White House, and the President [Franklin D. Roosevelt] invariably requested that Gershwin classic 'It Ain't Necessarily So,' a favorite of his." There would be other presidential performances. Jane sang at the inauguration of Roosevelt's successor, fellow Missourian Harry S. Truman, and she also sang for Dwight D. Eisenhower, the next president.

There were other command appearances as well. Some were for the National Press Club in Washington, D.C. There was an all-Gershwin program at New York's Lewisohn Stadium, a concert at Carnegie Hall, and one in Palm Beach for a children's benefit, to name a few. The Palm Beach program had particular significance for Jane. It was there that she met George Gershwin.

Gershwin had long been recognized as a premier songwriter and Jane had been singing his songs for some time. When the two met, Gershwin had a special request of her. It was 1934, and he was writing the music for *Porgy and Bess.* Jane wrote: "He asked me to introduce its lullaby 'Summertime' over the air. He promised that if I did he would allow no other artist to sing it for a year and he kept his word." Over the years, many other artists have sung this song, but few with the feeling and emotion that Jane brought to it.

Jane's career continued to move forward. After the repeal of Prohibition in 1933, American nightclubs, no longer labeled speakeasies, became respectable. They served good food and drink and began hiring the best performers of the day to attract customers. Jane began her nightclub career in 1940 at a country club in Evanston, Illinois. Then came Chicago's Chez Paree, Miami's Copacabana, and New York's Versailles.

It seemed as if everything was going Jane's way. The days

when she designed and made her own stage clothes, as she did during her early career in show business, were over.

I was no longer wearing the sequin costume and little sequin shoes to match. I was wearing the exquisite elegant gowns of Valentina in all their flowing classic grace. . . . I was by now the highest paid gal on the air. My income got to four figures a week and I was billed as "Park Avenue's Favorite Entertainer."
    I had a cover on Life!

Jane appeared on the cover of *LIFE* magazine on March 14, 1938. But while her professional life was on track, her private life showed signs of stress. Her marriage was in trouble.

Don became more involved in Jane's career as his own professional life faltered. Acting as Jane's manager, he took over more and more of the decisions that had to be made regarding Jane's show business choices. In actuality, the William Morris Agency was guiding Jane's career, and tension grew between Jane and Don as more success came her way. Jane wanted to keep the marriage intact. According to newspaper stories, she twice went into retirement during the early years of her marriage in order to concentrate on jump-starting Don's stalled career. But those efforts failed, and Jane went back to work for economic reasons, returning to nightclubs, radio, recordings, and the musical theater. Financially, her marriage was saved, but in reality it was falling apart.

Jane's performing schedule would soon change as she went from "the bright lights of Broadway to a theater I knew nothing about, the dark stage of the European conflict." World War II would affect millions of lives, as it did Jane's. The war would crush many but not defeat them, including Jane. Yet as she wrote, "life for me was never to be the same again."

7. Patriotism and Disaster

As war clouds began to gather around the world in the late 1930s and early 1940s, Jane Froman was at the peak of her career. The turmoil in her personal life seemed to settle into a period of calm. Jane and Don purchased a house in Nyack, New York, on an eighty-five-acre estate that was near the homes of such theater people as actor Burgess Meredith, playwright Maxwell Anderson, and actress Helen Hayes. Known then as the First Lady of the American Theater, Hayes became another of Jane's lifelong friends. Years later, in 1965, after Jane retired, Hayes traveled to Missouri to accept Christian College's Distinguished Women of America Award.

Jane's pre-war performances seemed nonstop as she continued with her regular schedule of radio, recordings, and musical theater. In 1940, she appeared in a show at New York's Broadhurst Theater called *Keep Off the Grass*, as part of a cast that included Jimmy Durante, Ray Bolger, Ilka Chase, and Jackie Gleason. Once again, Jane made lifelong friends—Gleason and Durante would always be there for her. She would soon need the support of all of her friends.

The world was moving closer to war, and not even performers could ignore what was happening. Jane wrote: "As usual, all of us in show business were asked to do our bit. We went wherever the call was urgent or the cause needy." President Roosevelt asked America's entertainers to find time to do some shows for the "young men from all over the country . . . being crowded into Army camps in response to the draft." Ed Wynn and Jane, who later appeared together in a 1942 Broadway revue called *Laugh, Town, Laugh*, were

President Roosevelt asked entertainers to perform for American soldiers who were training in military camps across the country. Here, Jane performs at Camp Dix, New Jersey, on May 28, 1941. (Western Historical Manuscript Collection)

the very first entertainers to do a camp show for draftees, performing for the soldiers stationed at Fort Belvoir in Virginia. There would be other such shows for Jane, at places like Camp Dix in New Jersey and Camp Mead in Maryland. On April 6, 1942, at Fort Sheridan, Illinois, the U.S. Army named her an Honorary Master Sergeant.

In addition to keeping up the morale of American recruits, Jane worked in other ways to help defeat German Nazism and Japanese militarism. In November 1941, just prior to the attack on Pearl Harbor and the subsequent entry of the United States into the global conflict, Jane and composer

Richard Rodgers headed a group that traveled to Toronto to raise funds for the Canadian War Savings Drive. During a grueling twelve-hour stay, the Americans visited with Canadian soldiers and took part in a radio broadcast. After the December 7 bombing of Pearl Harbor by Japan, Jane increased her wartime activities. Having helped to collect more than $25,000 on her trip to Canada, she now concentrated on getting Americans to contribute to their own war bond drive. This effort brought her home to Columbia in the spring of 1942.

She arrived at the end of April and gave three "Victory Concerts," the culmination of a statewide drive to get all Missourians involved in the war effort. The performances, primarily of Gershwin songs, were held at Christian College, the University of Missouri, and Stephens College. According to a story in the *Columbia Daily Tribune* on April 15, the purpose was to "obtain voluntary pledges by every income earning citizen of Columbia to make regular purchases of War Bonds and Stamps."

Jane's appearances were successful. However, as she gazed out at the audience at each of the three concerts, she noticed they were all white. Segregation was practiced in many parts of the United States in the early 1940s, and the members of Columbia's African American community knew they would not be welcome at any of the scheduled Victory Concerts.

Jane was troubled by the irony of asking for money to defeat the horrors of fascism and militarism when one segment of the town's population was not free to attend her performances. Her friends remember that she was always aware of, and empathized with, those who were ignored, pushed aside, and made to feel that they were interlopers in society. She had felt at a very young age what it was like to be different, to be scorned, to be set apart from others; her childhood experiences taught her harsh lessons that she never forgot. When she saw an injustice, she tried to remedy it.

Jane's time in Columbia was short and filled with events, and she had to return to New York on May 3 to make record-

The War Savings Committee
of Columbia

VICTORY CONCERTS

featuring

Miss Jane Froman

and the

Burrall Symphony Orchestra

JAMES ADAIR, *Conductor*

Christian College, Wednesday, April 29

HONORABLE J. C. MILLER, President, Christian College
HONORABLE LLOYD KING, State Superintendent Schools

University of Missouri, Thursday, April 30

HONORABLE F. A. MIDDLEBUSH, President University of Missouri
HONORABLE R. E. LEE HILL, Alumni Secretary, University of Missouri
HONORABLE FRANK G. HARRIS, Lieutenant-Governor of Missouri

Stephens College, Friday, May 1

HONORABLE MERLE PRUNTY, Director, Extra Class Activities,
Stephens College
HONORABLE DAN NEE, Chairman, War Savings Committee,
State of Missouri

A program cover for the Victory Concerts that Jane gave in Columbia in the spring of 1942, autographed by her. Missing from the listing of scheduled performances is, of course, the performance Jane gave at Frederick Douglass High School for the African American community of Columbia. (Boone County Historical Society)

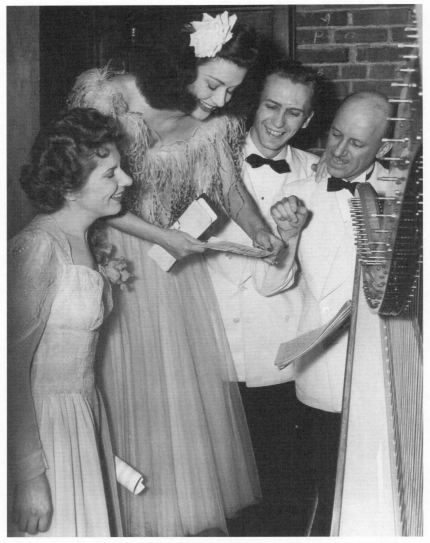

Jane and her fellow performers prepare for the fourth Victory Concert at Frederick Douglass High School in Columbia, Missouri, May 2, 1942. (Western Historical Manuscript Collection)

ings for the government the next day. However, she was determined to give another Victory Concert for Columbia's African American community. Without such an event, she believed, there could be no justification for asking all Americans to make the physical and financial sacrifices needed to win the war.

The concert would have to be held some place other than the campuses of the three colleges where African Americans felt unwelcome. It would have to be held within the segregated area of Columbia. Working with the Columbia War Savings Committee, the local African American community, and the faculty from Stephens College Conservatory, Jane hastily planned the fourth performance. On Saturday, May 2, an article appeared in the *Columbia Missourian* announcing that Jane would give one more Victory Concert that night. It was scheduled for 8:15 at Frederick Douglass High School.

Torrential rains and a severe hailstorm pelted Columbia that night and kept the concert from being sold out. Yet Jane's performance reflected the same talent and commitment to quality that she had shown in her three previous appearances. She could not end segregation in her hometown, but she wanted to treat the African American community of Columbia as she treated everyone else.

By December 1942, a year after Pearl Harbor, the United States was fully engaged in the war and the involvement of America's entertainers increased. It was no longer enough to perform stateside—American troops abroad needed entertainment too, and Roosevelt asked performers to volunteer to travel overseas. Jane was the first to wire her acceptance of overseas duty, responding within an hour of receiving the request. There was never any hesitation on her part to cheer up America's servicemen wherever they might be. She knew that the songs she would bring to those stationed abroad would raise morale. It could be her main contribution to the war effort. "It never occurred to me to ignore the request from FDR to head a unit scheduled soon to depart overseas," she wrote.

Whatever the need, Jane was there to aid the American war effort: "I sang beneath an enormous sign which read, 'Give Your Aluminum.' Pots and pans—stew pots, coffee pots, frying pans, roasting pans—all were piled in one vast heap in the middle of Times Square, with me on top waving enthusiastic congratulations to the housewives for ransacking their kitchens."
(Western Historical Manuscript Collection)

The man chosen to organize and coordinate this tour— called USO Camp Shows—was Jane's friend and agent, Abe Lastfogel, of the William Morris Agency.

Abe tapped talent for this project everywhere he could find it—from the Broadway theater, motion pictures, radio, night clubs. . . . He gave tirelessly of everything he had. For the stars no pay was involved. Nor for him. That's what kind of a guy he [was] and that's why everyone [loved] him, myself included.

While Jane waited for her assignment to travel to Europe, she continued performing at camp shows, military hospitals, and bond drives. She opened a new nightclub in New York—the Rio Bomba, where she appeared with Milton Berle, the future television pioneer whose friendship with Jane would span decades. The club became so popular that "patrons were literally lined up for blocks trying to get tables."

Jane arrived at the club every night "with bag packed, ready to take off, never knowing which performance would be my last." She finally received word on February 20, 1943, that she was to leave the next day. Jane met her six fellow USO troupe members at New York Municipal Airport at LaGuardia Field. All were in high spirits as they waited to board Pan American Airways' legendary seaplane, the *Yankee Clipper.* The plane, a Boeing 314, had been in service since 1939, when it made the first transatlantic passenger flight. The entertainers were not the only passengers on the flight: there were military officers, civilians, diplomats, and of course, crew members—a total of thirty-nine people. London was the destination, with various stops along the way, including one in Lisbon, Portugal.

Abe Lastfogel was at the airport to see the troupe off. He bade them "godspeed." What no one knew was that the plane would never arrive in London, and for Jane, as she wrote in her autobiography, "everything that I had worked for—money, jewels, possessions—everything I had come to believe in were to be wiped away with one swift, mad crash."

8. Death or Life

On the evening of February 22, 1943, the *Yankee Clipper,* the pride of Pan American Airways' overseas fleet, crashed into the freezing Tagus River near Lisbon, Portugal. Bodies both alive and dead mingled with the debris of the plane that was scattered over the river. As Jane wrote: "At 6:15 I'm sitting on the Yankee Clipper sitting beside the beautiful Tamara as we prepare to land in Lisbon. I suddenly find myself in the icy waters of the Tagus." At 6:46, the left wing of the sea-plane hit the water. One minute later, according to eyewitness accounts, the plane plummeted into the river.

Just before the crash, Tamara Drasin, another singer in the troupe, had asked Jane to trade seats. It was a fateful change—not only did Tamara die, but so did everyone else in that part of the plane except Jane. Of the thirty-nine people on board, only fifteen survived.

Jane remained in the dirty, bacteria-laden river for about an hour. One of the crew members surfaced close to her, and they gathered floating debris for support. After forty-five minutes, a launch approached, but it stalled before it could rescue them. Shortly afterward, another craft appeared, and they were pulled aboard. Jane described what happened next:

[I am] taken to a Lisbon hospital, which is unprepared to receive the injured and the dying. . . . I have no idea of the extent of my injuries, but at midnight they get to me. I sense that I am dying. They have stripped me of everything I possess, no identification, unable to communicate—in a foreign land where no one speaks the language and I don't understand a word. I have nothing left but what I have inside—shall we call it my soul. I am alone, utterly alone. I struggle to hold on.

Jane (fourth from left) *and other troupe members wait to board the* Yankee Clipper *on February 21, 1943. Second from the left is Tamara Drasin, who traded seats with Jane just before the crash. The pictures on the wall are of clipper seaplanes. (Western Historical Manuscript Collection)*

The injuries that Jane sustained were grave and numerous: a severe cut below her left knee, multiple fractures of her right arm, and a compound fracture just above her right ankle that nearly severed her leg. While being rescued, Jane had reached out with her good left hand to gently grasp her dangling right foot—she was afraid that as she was being lifted into the boat, it might be torn off.

There were other wounds: broken ribs, bruises, sprains, and cuts. Somehow, miraculously, her face was spared. Despite the gravity of her situation, Jane had to wait until the early morning hours of the following day for surgery. The most serious of all her injuries was the one to her right leg, which doctors thought might have to be amputated. She managed to convey to the physicians that if it came to amputation, she wanted to be told first. This was a request she would make through the years, as she continually faced the threat of losing her right leg.

Eventually, the survivors were transferred to a larger medical facility to convalesce. Jane was in Portugal for two months, "in casts from head to foot." Her husband, Don, arrived, with permission from President Roosevelt for Jane to return by plane to the United States, where she could receive the best medical care available. Since she was not able to fly, other arrangements were made to get her back home. She was placed on "a little freighter, 9 thousand ton Portuguese. I paid two thousand dollars to get home."

The voyage was anything but pleasant. In addition to being rocked by the rough Atlantic seas, the Portuguese steamer, the *Serapa Pinto,* came under attack from German submarines. Often, the torpedoes just narrowly missed the ship. Ultimately, in late April 1943, Jane arrived in Philadelphia. She was carried off the ship on a stretcher. Before being placed in a waiting ambulance, she asked to be lowered to the ground so she could touch America's soil for the first time in months.

Sadly, her ordeal did not end with her homecoming. "[I am] driven from Philadelphia in an ambulance to Doctors' Hospital in New York. I break down at last at the sight of white milk and bread. I shed my first tear and become violently hysterical." All of the emotions that Jane had been keeping pent up inside were finally released. It was the first time, but not the last, that she would shed tears over what had happened to her.

Once back in the United States, the full extent of the physical and emotional trauma that Jane had suffered became apparent. She found herself at a crossroads—she could choose the death that had been stalking her since the crash, or she could fight for her life.

Bewildered, crushed in body and spirit, I start to fight with only a flicker of life left in me.

Operation after operation, you lose track of them after a while, until you are reminded of the great sheaves of bills beside your hospital bed.

Twenty top doctors tell me I'll never walk again.
I know raw fear, terror and despair.
I'm told I'll have to lose my leg, that right foot that tapped its way
to the rhythm of song.
The furies take possession of my soul.

The public knew none of this, despite the fact that the
newspapers and magazines of the day followed the Froman
story in great detail. They reported on Jane's extensive injuries
and the many operations she endured. The media, however,
gave no hint of the inner turmoil Jane was going through.
But the reality was that she was struggling mightily and trying to summon the "fighting spirits" of her ancestors.

I try desperately to keep my leg and to keep my faith. I lose all my
belief, but somehow I manage to hold on to my leg.
But I'm crippled in spirit as well as body. The fight goes on—
physical—spiritual. I struggle to find a reason for it all. There must
be, there has to be some great purpose behind all of this. What is the
reason for the gnawing pain and the agony of mind?
Why was I alone spared of all the people in that section of the
plane? Why did that lovely girl Tamara insist I take her seat just
before the crash? Why is she dead and I'm alive, well, half alive.

Despite the torture and pain that consumed her, Jane
tried to keep her sense of humor. But the doubts and the
guilt were always there.

I've got to know! Why? Why should I suffer like this? Why should this
happen to me?
I'm bitter, rebellious, resentful. I'm terribly, terribly angry.
I struggle to understand why everything has been taken from me,
everything I'd worked for, when voluntarily and with no recompense of
any kind, I had left eagerly a life of excitement, glamour and success
to answer a call that I felt I must obey.
Stripped of everything right down to the bone—some of the bone
included—gradually, so, so gradually, I began to find the reasons.

I was to one day learn to walk again, and, oh thank God, to sing again. Some day, too, I could even talk. But right now I was bedridden and I was broke.

The journey from death back to life would not be easy for Jane. There were numerous operations; she would undergo crash-related surgery thirty-nine times before she was through. She later described the years immediately after the crash: "in casts, no money and out of a job, no one will give me work so I can pay those bills and liquidate the obligations incurred through my incapacities." There were times when bone grafts on her leg and arm did not heal correctly and had to be redone; when fragments of the plane, both wood and metal, would erupt from her skin; when larger fragments in her right arm, overlooked during initial operations, had to be surgically removed; when, after so much surgery, she required the attention of psychiatrists; and when she would spend "a lonely Christmas" in the hospital sharing a dinner of Chinese food with a fellow patient.

In contrast, there were better times. She remembered "Milton Berle and his bedside performances." Or Toots Shor, who owned a famous New York restaurant, sending over "hampers of beef" despite wartime shortages. Other "friends, fans, compassionate strangers, stars of stage, and screen and radio" were there for Jane. And so was someone else: the President of the United States, Franklin D. Roosevelt. Among the numerous problems that Jane confronted were the infections that she had contracted from the polluted waters of the Tagus. There was a new drug to fight such illness: penicillin. It was not in widespread use and it was in short supply because of the war. However, President Roosevelt gave orders that Jane was to receive this miracle drug. It most assuredly helped to save her life.

Jane had a very long way to go once she decided to choose life over death. Her battles would continue for years; in fact, she fought the injuries to her body and the furies in her soul until the day she died. One thing that carried her through was the joy she experienced on what she called that "great exciting day when I find my voice is not impaired." Indeed, it would be her extraordinary voice that would lead her back to life and back to her career.

9. *Recovery and a Promise Kept*

Getting back to work would prove to be a mixed blessing for Jane. It would take every ounce of energy she had—energy that she needed in order to recuperate. Yet working was a sign that she was on the road to recovery. Proving that she was capable of performing would help her find engagements, which, in turn, would enable her to pay her mounting medical bills. At least this was the plan. But, like many things in Jane's life, it did not work out as intended.

At first, all seemed to go well, as favorably as could be expected given Jane's condition. After a bone graft operation on her right leg in August 1943, her doctors suggested that work would be good therapy for her. Lou Walters (the father of television journalist Barbara Walters) and Don made plans to produce a revue called *Artists and Models.* Jane would be the star, and there would be other acts as well. To accommodate Jane, who was in a wheelchair and unable to stand or walk, discussions about the show and even rehearsals were held in the hospital, at times in Jane's room.

Jane Froman was once again on stage, barely eight months after the crash. In October 1943 the play opened on the road, in Boston. It was not easy for Jane to have the opening out of town, but she displayed courage and an indomitable spirit. She traveled by train to Boston. To board and exit her railroad car compartment, she had to be placed on a cot and pushed through the window. In Boston, the men who carried Jane dropped her onto the platform as they were lifting her out of the window. Fortunately, the only major damage was to Jane's cast, but the mishap was painful.

Rehearsing, in the hospital, for Artists and Models, *1943. (Western Historical Manuscript Collection)*

This would not be the only misfortune. "In the afternoon of the Boston opening I learn that Mama's husband has died of a stroke." Then, on opening night at the Boston Opera House, "a group of stagehands assigned to carry the 85-pound me and the 35-pound cast onto the stage dropped me to the floor in the wings as my number was being introduced." The show was stopped for a few minutes while Jane recovered. When she was sufficiently composed and the curtain was raised, the audience welcomed her with wild applause. Jane later recalled the emotion of that moment. "I receive an ovation from a standing audience as I finally get on stage. I try in vain to keep control of a weeping company and a wildly clapping, cheering audience for 20 minutes."

After the trial run in Boston, *Artists and Models* was ready for New York. Getting onto the stage remained difficult for Jane. She was carried on and off for each of her appearances in the show; on matinee days, that meant forty-four times a day. Eventually, she would learn to navigate on crutches and would be able to get about on stage herself. The tremendous effort it took for Jane to perform became known only later, and that was the way she wanted it. From *Artists and Models* to her last professional appearance in 1961, Jane never wanted anyone to feel sorry for her, or to come to a performance to see her leg. Rather, she always wanted the audience to come to hear her sing, and to judge her on her voice and nothing else. Although the New York critics praised Jane's performance in *Artists and Models,* they were not kind to the show, and it closed after six weeks.

Jane was in pain during the entire run of *Artists and Models*— her right leg had started to cause trouble even before opening night. When the show closed, she returned to the hospital for more surgery to have a bone fragment removed. This surgery brought to the fore yet another problem that Jane had to confront—her use of pain medication.

The injuries that Jane had sustained caused constant and unrelenting pain. Each setback, each additional operation, only made the situation worse. Her injuries and the twenty-five operations she endured from 1943 to 1949 often caused her to experience excruciating pain for long periods of time. Her doctors gave her medication to ease her suffering. But Jane grew concerned that she might find herself addicted to painkillers.

There is a difference, of course, between habituation and addiction. Jane habitually used drugs to ease her physical pain, and she welcomed whatever relief they brought. A person who is gripped by the need to use drugs, on the other hand, is an addict. Jane's doctors were cautious about the powerful drugs they were dispensing. Both they and, most particularly, Jane were mindful of the danger of her crossing the line into addiction.

Eventually Jane took the matter into her own hands. In January 1944, she went back into the hospital—not for surgery, but to rid her body of any remedies that could be addictive. Her timing was unfortunate, because shortly after this, she needed further surgery on her leg. But this time, by sheer determination, she recovered without the use of any pain medication.

All of these hospitalizations added to Jane's mounting medical bills. She needed to work, both financially and emotionally, no matter what the physical toll. She realized she could not perform for extended periods on Broadway because getting on and off the stage was too difficult. So, from late 1944 to mid-1945, she concentrated on radio and nightclubs.

Performing on radio was not a problem—the audience only heard her voice and did not see her wheelchair and crutches. Nightclubs, though, presented a dilemma. To handle it, a motorized piano-platform was devised. Before Jane appeared, the lights in the club would be dimmed. When the lights came back on, there was Jane on the platform, held in place by straps no one could see. The device was really a small moveable stage that the accompanist could navigate around the floor of the nightclub as Jane sang. Jane called these performances "night clubs on wheels."

She opened at Chicago's Chez Paree in November 1944, stayed there for two months, and followed that engagement with one at New York's Copacabana. It was a grueling schedule, since she did three shows a night. Time for her anguish and pain would have to wait—she needed the money. Jane would have continued this demanding routine had it not been for the wartime restrictions on electricity use, which in effect grounded her "night club on wheels."

Always resourceful, Jane found another way to work— she accepted an engagement at New York's Capitol Theater. For her performances there, which were five a day, Jane had to climb, with her leg brace and crutches, up "100 steps a performance to a platform on the stage." Now the singer, who

"Night club on wheels," with Frank Sinatra sitting on the piano. (Western Historical Manuscript Collection)

had already become a symbol of great bravery, undertook yet another challenge. She realized that if she could climb those hundred steps five times a day, she could "now complete the job I once set out to do." She decided to return to Europe and make the tour she had embarked on two years earlier.

Against doctors' orders, Jane once again responded to the call of the USO. Even though the war in Europe ended in May 1945, many homesick men were still stationed there and needed some morale boosting. That same month, in discomfort in a leg brace and on crutches, Jane sailed for Europe; there would be no plane trip this time. She traveled more than thirty thousand miles to six countries—France, Germany, Austria, Czechoslovakia, Luxembourg, and England—and gave ninety-five shows in three and a half months. Her gutsy appearances were an inspiration to all who saw her or heard her sing. The soldiers and Jane shared a special bond of understanding and sympathy that lasted a lifetime. There was an unspoken feeling among those World War II wounded that if a girl could do it, so could they. Jane was their inspiration, and one unit made her its pin-up girl.

The tour was cut short when Jane dislocated a bone in her back while mounting a stage in Austria; the injury forced her to return home to New York in the fall of 1945. Her homecoming was anything but joyous. Not only did her back have to heal, but she found out that she needed more surgery. In December, she was facing an operation for the removal of tumors from her leg. However, the night before the procedure, she left the hospital to attend the New York Newspaper Guild's annual Page One Ball, where she was named the most courageous entertainer of the year. After performing with jazz great Duke Ellington, Jane returned to the hospital and had the operation the next morning.

The following year, 1946, was no less difficult for Jane. When she was not in the hospital, she was performing in nightclubs, often in great discomfort, to earn money for upcoming medical procedures. "I hear with consternation the grafts are

Pin-up girl picture for the 900th M.H.S.P. (military hospital ship). Jane's inscription reads: "Thank you for the honor of being your pin up girl! Continued good health and good fortune." Throughout her 1945 European tour, Jane always asked audiences: "Is there anyone from Missouri?" If there was, she would invite him onto the stage to sing with her. (Western Historical Manuscript Collection)

not going right. The grafting of my leg and arm are unsuccessful—no union between bones. Operations have to be done all over again." To get ready for the upcoming surgeries, Jane and her mother traveled to Coral Gables, Florida, to build up her "health for the ordeal." As her strength returned, Jane remained worried about her finances. "I need more money for more operations—night clubs in Florida are the answer. [Singer] Sophie Tucker and [comedian] Joe E. Brown cancel their dates so I can have their jobs to earn the money."

In 1947, her nightmare continued—there were still rough times ahead for her. However, what Jane could not have known then was that 1947 would be the beginning, both medically and personally, of better things to come. It all began in February. After having tolerated outdated medical treatment for years after the crash, she finally found a new orthopedic surgeon, Dr. Mather Cleveland, who had acquired extensive surgical experience during World War II and knew the latest medical techniques. He explained to Jane that she would need five separate operations to have any chance that new bone grafts would save her right leg. She entered St. Luke's Hospital in New York. The plan was for her to be there for six months—it turned out she stayed eight. Jane was "torn with worry" about her health and because "money again gives out."

Financially, though, things got better. Jane's agent, Abe Lastfogel, came forward with a large check on behalf of the William Morris Agency that helped with her medical costs. Physically, Jane took a turn for the worse. She nearly died from shock following the surgeries, and she again developed osteomyelitis, an inflammation of the bone. This insidious infection is caused by staph bacteria entering the bone or bone marrow. It is accompanied by high fever, chills, nausea, and great pain. Jane had been infected when, with a myriad of exposed and broken bones, she was thrown into the germ-ridden Tagus River. The illness returned periodically, and it became something that she dealt with continually after the crash. While this particular outbreak was brought under control, Jane's situation looked bleak.

Again the doctors insist I lose my leg, even the dear Doctor Mather Cleveland who has been with me all the way agrees that hope is gone, my leg must go.

I denounce them all. Stubborn and defiant, I will not let them cut off that leg.

Mama takes a little flat nearby. She refuses to believe (even to herself) I'm to be crippled, or even left with scars and braces. Little did she know! She keeps that stiff upper lip, comes daily to the hospital and goes to music classes regularly at the Juilliard Foundation.

The leg remains.

Jane's defiance, determination, and fortitude, character traits that were honed in her childhood, helped her now. She kept her right leg, although she would wear a leg brace for the rest of her life. Soon, another problem would affect her. While she was devoting all of her energy and strength to coping with the painful procedures necessary for her recovery, her marriage to Don Ross was nearing an end.

10. *Breakdown and Renewal*

When Jane boarded the *Yankee Clipper* in February 1943 for that fateful trip to London, her marriage was already in trouble. When she returned to the United States, broken in body and spirit, her condition only made a bad situation worse.

Don, who considered himself to be Jane's manager/agent (although in reality it was the William Morris Agency that guided her career), was a man without a client when Jane could not perform. He considered it his responsibility to get her on her feet and working as soon as possible; thus he had arranged her role in *Artists and Models* shortly after the plane crash and long before she had recovered from her injuries. Because of the situation, Don took over the sole and exclusive supervision of Jane's medical treatment. Being too sick to object, she acquiesced.

One of the by-products of war is the advance of medical information and techniques. This was certainly true during World War II, but the doctors that Don turned to were not yet familiar with the best and latest medical knowledge that had come about as a result of the war. Consequently, Jane suffered needlessly, as one operation after another had to be redone. In all likelihood, her recovery was delayed immeasurably because of obsolete medical practices. Whenever she felt strong enough to offer a suggestion that different doctors be used, Don outvoted her.

Another problem was that he turned more and more to alcohol, and Jane found that she could rely on him less and less. Often he would go out at night, leaving her alone in their apartment and fearful: What would she do in case of fire or some other emergency? How would she manage to get out of the apartment? In truth, her marriage to Don was becoming increasingly intolerable to her.

Complicating the circumstances was the fact that Jane had a suitor. He was John Curtis Burn, Pan American Airways' fourth officer on the *Yankee Clipper.* Before the tragedy, John had been a fan of Jane's and had seen her perform at the Roxy Theater in New York. A crew change had put him aboard the ill-fated plane. When the plane plunged into the black waters of the Tagus River, he was the crew member who surfaced close to Jane and stayed with her until they were rescued. John's numerous injuries, while severe—including broken vertebrae— were not as critical as Jane's. Their recuperation in Portugal had brought them together, and now Jane, trapped in an unhappy marriage, was attracted to John and he to her. However, Jane felt nothing could come of it; she believed in the sanctity of marriage and felt her relationship with John was the chance result of a tragic accident.

John returned to the United States about two weeks after Jane. He called her at the hospital and came by for visits. Rather quickly, it became apparent that the attraction they had developed for one another in Portugal was not going to go away now that they were both home. At first, John respected Jane's wish to remain loyal to her husband. Moreover, Jane was in no condition to be making romantic decisions; she was fighting her way through one operation after another and was constantly looking for singing engagements. Nevertheless, as her marriage crumbled and Don became less reliable, Jane turned more and more to John. She called John's name when she came out of anesthesia after surgery, and he sent flowers to her club openings. Before Jane left for Europe in 1945, however, the two agreed not to see each other any more. Jane resolved to remain steadfast in her marriage, even as it fell apart.

When Jane returned from her USO tour in September 1945 and faced more surgery, Don proved to be even less of a

Wedding to John Burn, March 12, 1948. The cross that Jane is wearing was her only possession to survive the plane crash. (Western Historical Manuscript Collection)

comfort to her than before. She felt more and more lonely as she faced unrelenting operations, disappointments, and pain alone. Once more, she turned to John, and they agreed to meet. In the spring of 1946, Jane traveled to Florida, as she often did to regain her strength in the sand and sun. John, his injuries healed, had resumed flying for Pan American Airways in March of that year and was stationed in Miami. When he saw how unhappy Jane was, he insisted she divorce Don and marry him. Jane was still hesitant, not because she did not love John, but because she did not want to burden him with an invalid. She had no way of knowing if she would lose her leg. John dismissed such thoughts, saying he loved her, not her leg. But the same stubbornness that saw Jane through all of her troubles proved too strong for John to break. For the time being, she refused John's pleas.

When Jane returned to New York, however, she finally stood up to Don. She demanded a new orthopedic surgeon, found Dr. Cleveland, and underwent the painful series of operations, with their complications, that debilitated her for much of 1947. During her eight-month hospital stay, Don was barred from visiting her because he was often drunk and would call at all hours of the night. John, though, was there for Jane, having arranged a temporary transfer to New York. Finally, Jane realized that the marriage of Froman and Ross was over.

Jane was released from the hospital in October 1947. She filed for divorce from Don and received it the following February. One month later, on March 12, 1948, Jane married John Burn, "braces, crutches, and all." The wedding took place at John's house in Coral Gables, Florida. With her health finally improving—"I'm well again and on my feet—maimed, of course, but able to go on with my work"—and with a happy marriage, it seemed that Jane's life was finally back on track after so many difficult years.

John arranged to be transferred to New York permanently and the newlyweds found an apartment. Jane was on the radio once again, and was able to do her nightclub act, walking on and off the stage without her crutches. She was, she wrote, "in high gear." Soon, though, "the aftermath" began.

The eight-month hospital stay in 1947, with its surgeries, infection, and near-death episode, had tested Jane's commitment to avoid pain medication whenever possible. In May 1949 she entered the hospital yet again, this time for a nerve block on her right leg, which doctors thought would lessen her need for medication. The procedure was not very successful, and the withdrawal of painkillers was an ordeal for Jane. Nonetheless, she was determined to succeed and she left the hospital in June, proud of her achievement.

To recuperate from her latest ordeal, Jane vacationed the summer of 1949 at Fire Island, New York. Impatient to regain her strength, she overexercised, causing an abscess on her right leg to open. She was terrified that the dreaded osteomyelitis had returned. It had not, and her doctors rapidly brought the new infection under control. However, Jane's psyche could not be restored so quickly. "I know I'm losing my grip. Suddenly with little warning 'battle fatigue,' breakdown, crackup. I know I have to get help, expert help." After years of fighting crushing injuries, cheating death, years of stubborn determination to recoup from setback after setback, Jane was so weary that her emotions were a shambles, and she suffered a mental breakdown. As her body was mending, it was now time for her spirits to heal.

In September 1949, Jane and John journeyed to the famous Menninger Clinic in Topeka, Kansas. In an article intended for a magazine, Jane later wrote, "I was positive I was going to be there all of my life." Broken in spirit as she was, she saw no way out; she felt she had hit bottom.

At the clinic Jane's routine consisted of taking classes in painting, ceramics, and other arts and crafts. There were social activities and daily talks with doctors; Dr. William C. Menninger took a special interest in Jane. In typical Froman fashion, she tackled each task with determination. She wanted to get well and made great strides toward that end. Within three months, her physical condition improved to the point where she discarded her crutches and cane, played some golf, and danced, even with her heavy leg brace. She began sleeping and eating better for the first time since the crash. As her physical condition improved, so did her mental outlook. Her self-confidence returned, and as it did, her stutter began to lessen. "I [found] through my psychiatric experience that my speech is improving." When John visited Jane at Christmas, he was astonished at the improvement in both her physical and emotional state.

While Jane was at the clinic, she learned techniques that permitted her to control her stuttering while performing. It took great effort and concentration to do this. In reality, the stuttering never left, and when Jane was off stage, in private and among friends, she never hid her problem.

Jane did not stay at the clinic for the rest of her life, as she thought she would when she checked in, but she was there for six months. In March 1950 she went home, her body and soul mended. There would always be continuing health problems resulting from the crash. Now, though, Jane was stronger. Menninger had altered her outlook on life. Once again she had come to a turning point: she could wither and die, or she could fight the demons within her and choose life. Once again, she chose life. As she left the clinic, the old Froman spirit returned. She wanted what a cruel fate had taken from her—she wanted her career back, not just a few singing appearances to pay her medical bills. She wanted once more to be the top female performer of her time. Jane Froman was on her way back.

With their heavy work schedules, John and Jane liked to relax whenever they could. Here Jane demonstrates her golf swing with her cane and a pinecone as John looks on. (Western Historical Manuscript Collection)

11. Comeback and Court

The decade of the 1950s was a time of extreme opposites for Jane Froman. There were years of tremendous highs and years of profound lows. It was as if her career was a shooting star—she began the decade blazing across the entertainment scene, shining brightly, only to burn out and fade away in the end.

Fresh from her stay at the Menninger Clinic, Jane was eager to reestablish herself in the world of show business, and she wasted no time in doing so.

At last through the power of speech so long denied me, I am able to introduce in my own words my new act when I return to work and open the new Persian room at the Plaza [in New York City]. Jubilant and astounded, Dr. Cleveland is present—with tears rolling down his cheeks, saying over and over again, saying "My God, I would never have believed it."

It seems that for Jane, being able to talk for herself while performing was as important as healing from her physical injuries. After the Persian Room, other engagements quickly followed.

It was fitting that Jane's first television appearance was on Milton Berle's *Texaco Star Theater.* Milton and Jane had been close friends for years, and after the plane crash, he was often at her bedside in the hospital trying to cheer her up. After performing on Berle's show, Jane was a guest on other top-rated television programs, but the appearance she was most proud of was her stint as host of Ed Sullivan's *Toast of the Town.*

Jane with Susan Hayward on the movie set of With a Song in My Heart.
(Western Historical Manuscript Collection)

When Ed Sullivan goes to Europe I'm able to MC his entire Sunday TV show, even when the intercom breaks down. I deliver cue after cue for four numbers, four acts, and sing my own songs. The joy of being able to speak at last.

Not to mention the joy of being able to sing professionally again: "Oh, thank God, to sing again."

Everything seemed to be falling into place for Jane. Once more she was appearing in nightclubs, including those in the nation's newest entertainment mecca, Las Vegas. There, in the desert, the hotels paid her as much as $17,500 a week. While she was starring at the Flamingo Hotel, talks began about bestowing on Jane a rare accolade—a movie of her life. Film companies including Paramount, MGM, Warner Brothers, and Twentieth Century Fox expressed an interest in such a project. Actually, this was not Jane's first encounter with Hollywood.

In 1933, Jane Froman was cast in a short film for Warner Brothers called *Kissing Time.* A few years later, in 1935, Jane starred in another Warner Brothers production, the feature film *Stars over Broadway.* Her third and last movie had been *Radio City Revels,* in 1938, for RKO. Jane received good reviews for each of these films. In order to be a movie star, however, more than physical beauty and a wonderful singing voice were required: it was necessary to be able to speak clearly without stumbling over dialogue. Jane tried mightily to do that in each of her three movies and, in a limited fashion, she succeeded. Her efforts were not enough, though, to sustain an entire movie, let alone a film career. Jane might have been a star in silent movies, but by the time Hollywood wanted her, that era was long past.

When the movie studios showed interest in her in the 1950s, it was not Jane Froman they wanted; they sought instead the rights to her life story. Jane met with the competing studios and chose Twentieth Century Fox to make her movie biography. Filming on *With a Song in My Heart* began

Jane gave a concert on the steps of St. Clair Hall in 1951 to celebrate the one hundredth birthday of Christian College. (Western Historical Manuscript Collection)

in Hollywood in 1951. Susan Hayward played Jane, and Jane was thrilled at Hayward's selection. Jane served as technical advisor, but was more than a consultant on the film: she became Hayward's singing voice. Through the art of dubbing, Jane sang all of the songs, and the movie soundtrack topped the charts for weeks. *With a Song in My Heart* opened in New York on April 4, 1952—Easter time—at the Roxy Theater, where Jane had performed. Audiences loved it, and the reviews were enthusiastic. It received five Academy Award nominations, including one for Hayward, and won in one category, best musical score.

Ironically, as the movie was released, tragedy struck Jane yet again. "Two days after the opening, my husband is in another plane crash." By now John Burn was a captain, flying the Caribbean route for Pan Am. His plane went down off the coast of San Juan, Puerto Rico; fifty-two people lost their lives, but once again John was spared. Jane rushed down to Puerto Rico, by plane, to be with her husband.

Jane wanted to retire after the release of her film biography. Two trips home to Columbia had probably increased that longing. She and John had traveled to Columbia in 1948 when she was honored as "Coming Home Queen" during Homecoming Week at the University of Missouri, the first time Jane had been back to Missouri since the plane crash. A few years later, she returned to help her alma mater, Christian College, celebrate its centennial in 1951. On both visits, everywhere she went, whether it was a homecoming rally at the university's Jesse Hall or the concert she gave on the steps of Christian College's St. Clair Hall, Jane was praised, applauded, and admired.

As tempting as the prospect of retirement was, Jane put such thoughts aside and continued performing; she gives no indication in her autobiography of the reason for that decision. Along with her usual venues of nightclubs and recordings, Jane's career took a new turn when CBS offered her a television show of her own. The program debuted in 1952 and was

Jane loved to dance. After the crash, doctors were concerned whether she would survive, let alone walk again. When her television career started, one of the things Jane wanted to do was dance. She practiced her routine in private, and then, to the surprise of everyone, on her first broadcast she danced with a soldier. In this photo, she dances with a cast member on another broadcast of the show. (Western Historical Manuscript Collection)

called *USA Canteen;* it catered to servicemen, who always had a special place in Jane's heart. Subsequently renamed *The Jane Froman Show,* it became more of a musical variety program.

In 1953, Jane received a letter from the mother of a young man serving in the Korean War; she was looking for solace and support. Jane turned the letter over to her songwriters, and as a result, they composed "I Believe." It was a hit—the first song introduced on television to become popular. Moreover, Jane and the writers received a special honor, the Christopher Award. This award is still given yearly by the Christophers to those in the media who "affirm the highest values of the human spirit."

Jane remained a fixture on television until her show ended in 1955. In addition to her own program, she made guest appearances on other television shows, recorded albums, gave concerts, and performed in nightclubs. Audiences wanted to hear her sing. She wrote that her career "zoomed," and she was once again in demand as one of America's most popular female vocalists. Jane had taken back what fate had snatched from her in 1943. She had cheated death, survived almost too many operations to count, and spent years in and out of hospitals. She had regained her career by sheer will, stubbornness, and determination, and, through it all, acquired the respect and admiration of everyone who knew her.

Organizations and institutions bestowed honors upon Jane for all she had accomplished and for the inspiration she was to others. One tribute that Jane especially cherished came in 1952 from the Cincinnati Conservatory of Music, where she had been a student almost twenty-five years earlier. The conservatory conferred upon her an honorary doctorate for her accomplishments in music. Anna was at the ceremony.

Mama walks in the procession in cap and gown (I see to that) with a triumphant smile on her face, convinced at last I do believe that her daughter has amounted to something in music. I am able to present a scholarship to be used by some young student who, like myself, wants to study music without money enough to finance it.

Jane receiving an honorary degree from the Cincinnati Conservatory of Music in 1952. (Western Historical Manuscript Collection)

Awards were gratifying, but Jane's financial needs continued. Soon after the *Yankee Clipper* crash in 1943, she and other survivors had sued Pan American Airways for damages, including medical expenses and the pain and suffering that each endured. However, the "small fine print on the back of every airplane ticket—the Warsaw Convention," doomed their efforts to failure. In 1929, a number of countries had agreed that in case of international airline disasters, passengers would be able to collect only $8,300 in compensation. The United States consented to this convention in 1934. Although reimbursement amounts today are notably higher—in 1966 the limit was raised to $75,000—the rationale then was that people who flew in a plane knew the risks they were taking and if an accident occurred, the airlines should not be held responsible. The only exception was if it could be proved that there was pilot negligence. But that was almost impossible to do, because what pilot would deliberately cause injury or death to himself and others?

By the time of the *Yankee Clipper* crash, $8,300 was by no means a realistic settlement amount. Jane's medical bills through the years amounted to hundreds of thousands of dollars, and that does not include her ongoing expenses for nurses, special shoes, braces, prescriptions, and other costs. She only wanted what was fair, and $8,300 in compensation was not fair.

Jane sued for damages in the summer of 1944. From then through the end of her legal battles in 1953, she did not win a single case she brought in court. The prevailing opinion was that in accepting her plane ticket with the "small fine print" of the Warsaw Convention printed on the back, she had accepted the risk of flying and knew what her compensation would be in case of a tragedy. Jane's only hope was to show deliberate pilot error. Her lawyers had to demonstrate, beyond a doubt, that the pilot of the *Yankee Clipper*, Captain Robert O'D (Rod) Sullivan, a Master Ocean Pilot, failed to follow the proper water landing procedures as mandated by Pan Am when he attempted to land on the Tagus River.

In a well-publicized trial in New York City in 1953, Jane's final lawsuit against Pan Am was covered by all of the media. Her attorneys were working against the legal odds—they had to provide evidence that Sullivan had made a mistake, and they sought a settlement of $2.5 million. That was an unheard-of sum in those days, and it was also unusual for an individual to sue a large corporation for damages. Some survivors of the crash had settled earlier for the $8,300 as prescribed by the Warsaw Convention. Jane's request looked absurd to the uninformed, but none of the other survivors had been as severely injured as she or suffered such lifelong and debilitating injuries.

In the courtroom, Jane told of her harrowing experiences during and after the crash; airplane specialists gave expert testimony about the lax procedures of the *Yankee Clipper* pilot; Jane's doctors gave sworn accounts about her massive injuries; and John Burn took a leave of absence from Pan Am so that he could take the stand to give evidence in the case. In the end, despite having excellent lawyers, Jane lost. She was awarded $9,050—$8,300 plus $750 for lost luggage. It was a miscarriage of justice that she felt very deeply. In 1962, Congress awarded Jane and two other survivors of the crash $20,000—a symbolic gesture that did not lessen Jane's disappointment in the outcome of her case. Years later, she wrote, "How wrong I still feel the whole thing is."

Her misfortunes continued. While her career was back on track, once again her personal life was not. With Jane and John citing conflicting career demands, their fairy-tale marriage ended in divorce in 1956. John always seemed to be flying off to distant destinations while Jane was performing somewhere else. This was the public reason given for the break-up. But if Jane and John's marriage was in trouble because of their competing professions, why did Jane not try retiring from show business, as she had done twice during her marriage to Don Ross? Whatever the reason, Jane and John parted as friends. While both would remarry, it is a widely held belief among those who knew Jane that John remained the love of her life.

Thus, the mid and late 1950s brought Jane a series of losses and disappointments—the loss of her case against Pan Am; the cancellation of her television show; the end of her marriage; and then, in 1957, another health crisis: "all of a sudden, a slipped disk."

Again, the combination of physical pain and emotional stress took a toll. It was not until two years later that Jane felt ready to try to make yet another comeback. Even though she had some thoughts of leaving show business, Jane put together a new nightclub act in 1959 that received very favorable reviews. Jane Froman seemed to be in top form once more. However, her life was about to change again.

I begin to think is it all worth it. Is this what I really want out of life. Is this all there is to it? Two more operations. I ponder and ponder.

My heart tells me I don't belong here anymore. I slowly begin to sort my values, to take stock in life and what I really want in it. I've given my profession everything I have, and it has given me everything it has—fame, fortune. Surely, there is something more to living than all this—just a series of repeat performances. An honest artist, I feel I'm not able to give everything I have anymore. I make my plans and come to my decision.

12. *Home and Retirement*

In May 1961, after thirty-four years in show business, Jane Froman decided that it was time to go home.

To Jane, home was always Columbia, Missouri. She was leaving behind a career that had taken her to the very top of her profession as one of the most popular vocalists in the entertainment business. That was all behind her now. She was going home to the place she loved. The question was whether it would be a temporary return or a permanent retirement. Would Jane Froman really leave show business forever?

Years of operations, recuperations, and comebacks had sapped Jane's strength. Her last setback, a slipped disk, had taken her two years to overcome. Finally, just when she thought she had recovered, when she had launched still another return to her career, Jane learned that she needed more surgery. This time it was not her back, not her "bad" right leg, but her left leg, her "good" leg, that needed attention to relieve the pain she was experiencing in her knee. Jane decided to have the operation in Columbia. She canceled scheduled engagements, said good-bye to her friends, put her belongings in storage, closed up her New York City apartment, and headed home. Once more, she was exhausted both emotionally and physically.

Jane returned to the home of her mother, who had been a widow since 1943. Anna was living in a small bungalow that she had purchased in 1945 after her husband's estate was settled and she began teaching at Stephens College. Jane's world, which once included the glitz and glamour of the finest hotels, restaurants, theaters, and homes, was now one room in her mother's modest house. However devastating that must have been for Jane's sense of self-esteem, she had no choice. At age fifty-three, she had little money and no place else to go; she needed to get well before she could make any decisions about the rest of her life.

Jane planned to spend part of her convalescence taking art classes at the University of Missouri. Like the musical talent she inherited from her parents, Jane also had the ability to paint, a skill she believed came from her grandmother. Years later, Jane wrote that "in my Columbia dining room I am proud indeed of the gold-rimmed punchbowl set strewn with pink and white roses, and I cherish a pitcher for hot chocolate, sprinkled with violets [that Grandma Barcafer] painted with great delicacy and taste." While recovering from previous surgeries, Jane had discovered her gift for painting. Norman Rockwell judged her a "rare talent" and offered her a scholarship, if she ever wanted it, to his art school.

Jane intended to enter the university in the fall of 1961 after her knee surgery, but once again illness got in the way. This time it was a bout of pneumonia that delayed her plans. Frederick Shane, chairman of the art department, wrote to Jane and told her not to worry, that whenever she was "ready to start we will be glad to see you." Once recovered, Jane did begin art classes in the spring of 1962. She wrote of Anna's reaction to her enrollment in college courses: "I go back to school at the University of Missouri, where I once failed, and become an honor student. Mama is proud of me at last and calls everyone in town."

In addition to recovering her health and taking art classes, Jane set out to renew old acquaintances and friendships now that she was back in Columbia. One person of particular interest to her was Rowland Haw Smith. Smitty, as everyone called him—except Jane, who always called him Rowland—was a newspaperman with the *Columbia Daily Tribune.* He and Jane had attended the University of Missouri's journalism school at the same time. When Jane traveled to Europe in 1945,

Jane taking an art class at the University of Missouri, 1962. Instructing her is Douglas Hansen, professor of fine arts and former chairman of the art department. (Columbia College)

Smitty was one of the lucky soldiers who saw her perform. They met there, and Jane wrote his name and address in her journal. Now, upon her return to Columbia, they began seeing each other.

Smitty's wife, Ann, had died not quite a year before he resumed his friendship with Jane. After dating for some months, he proposed to Jane after they had attended a mutual friend's New Year's Eve gathering. Jane accepted, and she and Smitty were married several months later on June 20, 1962, at the First Presbyterian Church in Columbia.

Whether she had planned it that way or not, Jane was now permanently retired from show business. Her professional career was over; she was Jane Froman Smith, housewife. This was a role she had always desired but never seemed to be able to achieve. Retirement from show business did not mean retirement from life, however. Jane was to be busier than ever. Keeping still and staying quiet were just not in her nature. Charitable works, social activities, awards and recognitions, and a brief brush with performing again would fill her days and years in Columbia.

Smitty and Jane on their wedding day, June 20, 1962. A few weeks before her wedding, Jane had traveled to New York to purchase items for her trousseau and to visit with old friends. (Western Historical Manuscript Collection)

13. *Giving Back and Arrow Rock*

After a honeymoon at the Lake of the Ozarks, Jane and Smitty returned to Columbia, and Jane busied herself with establishing their home. She enjoyed collecting antiques and cooking, especially Italian foods. Soon, other activities followed.

Jane always had a special fondness for children, even though she never had any of her own, and she believed in giving something back to society. These interests came together after her stay at the Menninger Clinic. While there, Jane worked with emotionally disturbed children. She interacted with them, even singing to some as she rocked them to sleep. Thereafter, trying to ensure that children had access to good mental health care became a lifelong undertaking for her.

To realize her goal, she had established the nonprofit Jane Froman Foundation in April 1956. It was formed to support the activities of the Southard School, a part of the Menninger Clinic that treated emotionally disturbed children. The purpose of the foundation was to raise money for buildings and to pay professionals to work with young patients whose parents could not afford such care. Jane became president of the foundation, and she persuaded some of the leading entertainers of her day to serve on its board.

Fund-raising for the foundation was a high priority for Jane. Both before and after her retirement, she encouraged her fan clubs, which had sprung up around the country with the release of *With a Song in My Heart,* to contribute funds. Jane matched the amount of money they raised, donating the total to the Southard School. Her involvement was so extensive that she was elected to several terms as a trustee on the Menninger

the story

of the

Jane Froman

foundation

The cover of the brochure for the foundation that Jane established to help emotionally disturbed children. The work of this charity was always an important part of her life. (Western Historical Manuscript Collection)

Foundation's board of governors. After she retired, Jane often attended board meetings in Topeka. Dr. William C. Menninger expressed his appreciation for Jane's commitment, saying, "I am grateful to Miss Froman . . . for her deep interest in us and our program here for children." Jane's work on behalf of youngsters with emotional problems was conducted without much publicity or any self-promotion, and thousands of dollars were raised through her efforts. In 1977, she received a lifetime achievement award from the Menninger Foundation.

Jane knew from her own experiences how vital it was for adults as well to be able to obtain first-class medical attention for emotional troubles. She was ahead of her time, for in the 1950s and 1960s it was not as acceptable as it is today to seek help from mental health clinics. Conventional attitudes, however, never stopped her. Members of the Missouri Mental Health Association found Jane's participation so important to their efforts that they honored her with the association's annual award in 1971.

Mental health was not the only subject that caught Jane's attention. Years before she sustained her injuries, Jane was well aware of the needs of the physically disabled. She did benefits and visited hospitals, especially children's hospitals, whenever she could. After the plane crash, Jane took full advantage of her renewed fame and name recognition to become an outspoken advocate for the physically disabled. In 1953, while living in New York, she served as chair of that state's Easter Seal Campaign. When she returned to Columbia, she continued her relationship with the Easter Seal Society.

In September 1966, Jane was a featured speaker at the fortieth annual meeting of the Missouri Society for Crippled Children and Adults in Springfield, Missouri. Shortly afterward, the society announced that she had accepted the chairmanship of the 1967 Easter Seal Campaign for the state of Missouri. Such a responsibility meant that she would have to travel and speak to various groups around the state. Jane gladly accepted these duties, despite the weariness that came from frequent traveling and despite the fact that speaking before groups was not an easy task for her because of her stutter. As she once remarked to some friends: "Anyone who has been hurt or who has some injury is very dear to me. I can't explain it, but you know what I mean."

Jane used her own experiences to encourage others. She often remarked that she was seldom without pain, even decades after she received her injuries, and she urged those who were disabled to "get interested and involved in something." During the 1967 Easter Seal Campaign, Jane appeared with volunteers from all over Missouri, making radio and television appearances and attending meetings throughout the state. Her tenure as state chairman raised a record amount of money for the Missouri Easter Seal Society. So successful was she that four years later she was asked to once again take on some responsibility for fund-raising on behalf of the state organization. Jane accepted, and to honor her commitment she turned to an area that she knew best: show business.

On March 21, 1971, Jane Froman came out of retirement to act as hostess for a two-and-a-half-hour-long gala held in Kansas City on behalf of that city's Easter Seal chapter. The sixty-member cast of the locally produced musical *Showboat Hour* performed at the Municipal Auditorium, donating their services and all of the money raised to the Easter Seal Drive. Jane was elected that year to a three-year term on the board of directors of the Missouri Easter Seal Society, and continued to be active in that organization.

Jane was also involved with other organizations that promoted the needs of the disabled. The Rehabilitation Institute of Missouri named an award for Jane that is still given annually to the person who has done the most to overcome a disability. Jane spoke at a dinner in Kansas City on March 7, 1974, and presented the first of these achievement honors. As was her way, she took no credit for what she had accomplished; rather, she praised those who worked in the area of rehabilitation, calling them "beautiful people."

Also in 1974, Jane was the celebrity cohost for the Columbia portion of the national muscular dystrophy telethon. She worked with Paul Pepper, a local television personality. Not in the best of health, wearing a neck brace and using crutches, Jane nevertheless did all she could to raise funds for this cause. During the telethon, she continued a time-honored Froman custom: when she was on camera, there were no crutches to be seen and a scarf hid the neck brace.

Pepper found Jane to be "very kind, sweet, and talented" and "willing to do whatever" was needed to make the telethon a success. Jane's duties included doing promo spots to request donations and talking with people who came to the studio with contributions. Pepper had always been impressed with Jane, but after working with her, he said, he had great respect for her.

Those with musical talent needed support too, Jane believed. Because she so loved show business, she became associated with a project that permitted her to share her entertainment expertise with others. While working with the Easter Seal Society, she had met Jay Turley. After a career in the entertainment business, Turley had settled near Arrow Rock, Missouri, and began to work toward fulfilling his dream of establishing a music camp there. In 1969, he approached Jane with his plan. The idea intrigued Jane; it brought back memories of summers at the Seagle Music Colony with her mother and memories of those who had helped her when she was just starting out, particularly Fanny Brice. She cared deeply about helping young people prepare for a musical career. She believed that new artists sometimes rose so quickly that they knew little about stage presence. To help these aspiring performers, Jane agreed to be the music consultant for Turley's camp. Eventually, this venture would lead her to forsake her pledge that because of "artistic integrity" she would never perform in public again.

The association between Jane and Turley led to a series of musicals called *Steamboat Comin'*, which Turley wrote and

The Old Schoolhouse in Arrow Rock, Missouri, served as the site for the Jane Froman Music Center. (Photo by Ilene Stone)

produced to raise money for the camp. Jane took her job as music consultant seriously, and at times she became the unofficial director of the shows. She observed the rehearsals and, when necessary, would tighten up the programs to make them run more smoothly.

The first benefit performances for the camp were held on Memorial Day weekend in 1969 at Arrow Rock. The shows were financially successful and enabled Turley to purchase and remodel the Old Schoolhouse in Arrow Rock to use as a home for the camp. After the first show that weekend, Turley surprised Jane. He called her up to the stage and announced that he was naming the camp the Jane Froman Music Center.

Occasionally, Jane sang with the cast during the finale of the shows. While the cast performed, she waited across the street for her cue. A resident of Arrow Rock offered Jane the use of her living room, which she turned into her "dressing room." Jane's appearances on stage excited everyone, but the high point came in December 1969. Turley announced that a revised version of the musical *Steamboat Comin'* would be performed on December 20 and 21. These Christmas shows were to be called "A Party for Jane" and would feature Jane Froman singing solo in public for the first time in nine years.

Her professional pride made Jane work very hard to prepare for these concerts. After weeks of practice, she was gratified to know that "a little bit of the voice is still there," as she remarked to an interviewer for the *Columbia Daily Tribune* on December 19. The announcement that Jane would sing again attracted a great deal of attention. Two of the three performances were standing-room-only—bad weather prevented the third one from being sold out.

Jane sang "Good King Wenceslaus," "The Christmas Song," and "White Christmas." She received a standing ovation when she finished. One reviewer, writing for the *Tribune,* said that the event was "a magic moment" because there was "a direct personal experience between each member of the audience and the vibrant individual on the stage. Her voice filled the [Old Schoolhouse]. But more important than that, her personality filled the people." Jane told the audience, "I have never been so beguiled with anything in my life as I am with the music camp." She hoped that the camp could help young artists achieve their own magic moments, and worked hard to make it a success. Unfortunately, her dream was not fulfilled.

Those Christmas concerts were the last time that Jane performed for the music camp. In 1971 her alma mater Christian College, now called Columbia College, became involved with the project. It renamed the Old Schoolhouse the Jane Froman Arts Center and used it for student retreats and summer arts programs for area high school and college students. Jane continued to allow her name to be used in raising money for the center, and on June 16, 1972, the center held a celebration called Jane Froman Day. It was a fund-raiser to support the center and help sponsor the Arrow Rock Arts

After nine years of retirement, Jane performed in three Christmas concerts to raise funds for the music camp in Arrow Rock. Here she can be seen using her famed technique of a handheld microphone. (Photo by Carol Kennedy; from the collection of Carol Peck)

Series, which attracted nationally and internationally known artists to Arrow Rock for summer concerts. To Jane's undoubted disappointment, the fund-raising endeavors ended soon after the 1972 event, and the music camp and arts center never achieved her hopes for success. But Jane's public singing did not end with her Arrow Rock Christmas performances. She would sing one more time.

14. *Singing and Honors*

While Jane's holiday appearance and other activities at Arrow Rock were well publicized, another singing engagement was not. This one was not for charity; rather, it was a performance to honor the state she loved. The year 1971 was the 150th anniversary of Missouri statehood. To celebrate and commemorate that event, Jane gave her last public performance.

The program took place at the National Press Club in Washington, D.C., on October 28. The governor, other state officials and politicians, members of the press, and various friends of Missouri were in attendance. A troupe of five distinguished Missourians with various talents provided the entertainment. The troupe included Jane, whose aging, but still pleasing, contralto voice would add luster to some of her favorite songs. Jack Buck, the noted St. Louis sportscaster, was the master of ceremonies for the dinner show. Russ David, a well-known St. Louis musician, accompanied Jane and the other performers on piano.

Jane appeared toward the end of the nearly one-hour show. According to Gerald Hutton, one of the members of the troupe, "Jane was the big star" of the show, and her appearance was saved for last. When Buck introduced her, saying, "Ladies and gentleman, Jane Froman," the audience gave her a "tumultuous reception, a standing ovation." It was not easy physically for Jane to perform. For this presentation, as she did so many times before, she insisted on walking onto the stage without any aid. She stood in the curve of the piano for her medley of songs. Jane sang three numbers: "The Missouri Waltz," "Moanin' Low," and her signature song, "With a Song in My Heart." One audience member recalled that "the standing ovation at the end was better than the one at the start" of Jane's performance. For her last public singing appearance, it must have been very gratifying to Jane to hear the warm approval of the crowd.

Not only did she captivate the audience that night, but she also charmed her fellow performers. Buck recalled that Jane was "fantastic," and that the event was the "finest and most enjoyable night of my life because of her." He knew how hard it must have been for Jane to prepare for her performance; yet, as he recalled, she was "gracious and vivacious," a unique person "who would do whatever she had to do, even if it would not be easy." And he expressed a sentiment that was shared by all who knew Jane and admired her: that it was a "shame her talents were nipped by the crash," but nevertheless she was a "real professional."

Jane received many awards acknowledging her numerous contributions to the enrichment and betterment of others. None of these recognitions was as momentous to her as her election to the Missouri Academy of Squires in 1971. Founded in 1960, the academy honors Missourians for their accomplishments and contributions to the community, state, or nation. For obvious reasons, air travel had not been Jane's favorite form of transportation since 1943, through she did fly when necessary. On October 29, 1971, the day following her evening appearance at the celebration of Missouri statehood, Jane boarded a plane and flew to Missouri to be present at the Squires' induction luncheon. Governor and Mrs. Warren E. Hearnes hosted the event at the executive mansion in Jefferson City. The governor presented Jane with the Squires scroll, cane, and pin in recognition of her "generous giving of herself, her time, and her wonderful talent to everyone, but with an especial effort to those in need," calling her "an international star of radio, movies, and television and a champion of the arts." Missouri U.S. senator Stuart Symington wrote to congratulate her, and Jane responded modestly that

Jane and six others after their installation into the Missouri Academy of Squires on October 29, 1971. (Western Historical Manuscript Collection)

she did not deserve the "beautiful honor" but that it meant a great deal to her because it came from "fellow Missourians, home folks," which made it "doubly sweet and meaningful."

Jane was elected to the Squires in part because of her efforts to bring attention to men and women in uniform. Her love affair with the military began before the country entered World War II and continued all of her life. She always remembered with pleasure her performances for GIs: "Once you've done something like that, you're spoiled for any other audience. . . . The soldiers are marvelous." Jane had truly earned the title that *Variety*, the entertainment newspaper, had given her: "one of the original soldiers-in-greasepaint." Even after she retired, Jane often encountered members of the armed forces who expressed their appreciation for all that she had done to boost their morale.

Jane was constant in her patriotism. No matter what she may have thought about the country's involvement in Vietnam—and she acknowledged that it was "a different kind of war"—her concern was always for the GIs. She said that the only thing that would bring her out of retirement would be the opportunity to perform for the troops in Vietnam. The men "need entertainment," she said, "anything to get their minds off the war." Although she did not entertain the troops in Vietnam, she did visit veterans' hospitals in the United States, inspiring the patients with her own vitality, enthusiasm, and courage.

On March 28, 1968, the USO thanked Jane for her service to men and women in uniform, presenting her with a gold medallion that was designed and struck specifically for the occasion. The citation that accompanied the medallion read:

For her gallant pioneer effort to bring the sight and sound of home to our American troops in World War II, for her exceptional example of courage and devotion to duty despite personal sacrifice, this special citation is awarded to Jane Froman with great admiration and deep affection by the USO in the name of the American Armed Forces of three generations who have not forgotten.

The presentation took place in Dallas at the annual dinner of the USO national council. Besides leaders of the USO, those in attendance included generals, admirals, and other dignitaries. When Jane accepted her award, she gave tribute to her friend Abe Lastfogel, who was also honored that evening for his leadership in organizing the USO camp shows.

While Jane was thrilled with the USO award and others that came to her, she was not an "all work and no play" kind of person. She loved to have a good time, to go to a party, to enjoy herself, and to take pleasure in the life she fought so hard to keep.

15. Columbia and Jane

Once Jane became Mrs. Smith, the life of a homemaker was finally hers, and she made it an active and interesting one. She joined the circle of friends that Smitty had acquired during his years as a newspaperman and, later, as the associate director of the Office of Public Information at the University of Missouri. As a couple, Jane and Smitty also made new acquaintances together. When her health permitted, Jane had a full social calendar.

One of the things she enjoyed was sports. That was fortunate, because football was, and still is, a big part of the social scene in Columbia. Football Saturdays found Jane sitting in the stands of Tiger Stadium, gracefully wearing "the Black and Gold of Ol' Mizzou," a friend remembers. While Smitty was working up in the press box, Jane enjoyed watching the game and "chomping on a hot dog." Getting to her seat was not an easy task for her. If there was no friendly arm to lean on, she would climb up the steps with her crutches. After the game, she and Smitty would attend a cocktail party or go out to dinner with friends.

Jane did it all, wanting to miss out on nothing, including an activity that gave her great pleasure—dancing. It could not have been easy to dance while wearing a heavy leg brace, but Jane could and did, and not just occasionally. In 1964, she and Smitty joined a dance club that held regular events, and it was there they met Robert and Dorothy Benson. Smitty and Bob already knew each other as members of the Columbia Kiwanis Club, and Jane and Dottie soon became close friends.

According to Dottie, Jane "liked being with people. She

Taken in the early 1950s, this whimsical photo of Jane was one of Smitty's favorites. (Boone County Historical Society)

liked a good time." When she walked into a room, "everyone knew who she was, and they called her Jane." She never asked for special attention, Dottie said. She did not want to be treated as a celebrity, but just as another member of the club. She wanted to be like everyone else, to relax, and to enjoy herself, and she could do this with Dottie and Bob. The Bensons and the Smiths shared many good times together, even after Jane and Smitty left the dance club in 1975.

If a big-name entertainer came to Columbia to perform and Jane wanted to go, Smitty made sure she had the best seat in the house, usually in the front row. Bob Hope and Lawrence Welk were some of the artists she saw during her retirement years. They often introduced Jane, who would then acknowledge the audience's applause.

One occasion, a Henry Mancini concert, was particularly memorable. The concert was held at the Hearnes Center on the campus of the University of Missouri. The Bensons and another couple, the Robert Broegs, accompanied Jane and Smitty to the event. Halfway through the concert, Mancini said, "It is not my practice to dedicate songs to anyone in the audience, but I want to make an exception tonight to dedicate my next song, a love song, to Miss Jane Froman, a wonderful and talented great lady." He asked Jane to stand, and she did. After the performance, Jane and her party went backstage to thank Mancini for the tribute. Although public recognition was not something that Jane sought, she appreciated being remembered by other artists.

Other activities kept Jane busy. There were trips to Kansas City and St. Louis for social dinners and special occasions with friends. She held parties and receptions at her home to celebrate events such as her tenth wedding anniversary in 1972 or to support various projects in Arrow Rock. Old showbusiness chums visited, and Jane might cook one of her famous spaghetti dinners for them. She and Smitty played bridge with friends. The holiday season brought Thanksgiving dinners, Christmas celebrations, and New Year's Eve parties. And there were informal gatherings where Jane could relax and enjoy the company of close friends.

In addition to her social activities, Jane became part of many of Columbia's community organizations. She worked with the United Fund, the YWCA, and her sorority, Kappa Kappa Gamma; aided a community fund drive to help restore art objects damaged in a flood in Italy; and auditioned local voices for the New York Metropolitan Opera. To each venture, she brought her unending enthusiasm. Smitty once remarked that whenever Jane took part in a project, "she jumped in with both feet." The city of Columbia was grateful for all of her efforts, and in 1968 named her its Outstanding Woman of the Year. Two years later, the Alumni Association of the University of Missouri presented Jane with its Faculty-Alumni Award to recognize her distinguished service.

Christian College, Jane's alma mater, always held a spe-

Jane received the Distinguished Alumnae Award from Christian College in June 1963. As the photo shows, she could barely keep from crying. Before and after her retirement, the college was very special to her. (Columbia College)

In 1965 Jane was instrumental in bringing her friend Helen Hayes to Columbia to receive the Distinguished Women of America Award from Christian College for her outstanding work in American theater. (Western Historical Manuscript Collection)

cial place in her heart, and her support for the college did not stop with her retirement. In 1963, the National Alumnae Association of Christian College presented her with its Distinguished Alumnae Award. The citation honored Jane for her artistry as a singer, for the inspiration she provided to others throughout her career, for her courage, and for her service to the college alumnae association. Jane became a member of the board of directors of the National Alumnae Association and served as chairperson of its Records and Recognition Committee. She was instrumental in bringing prominent performers, including Helen Hayes, Vincent Price, and opera star Risë Stevens, to the campus to speak and receive awards. In 1976, the trustees of Columbia College invited Jane to become a member of its board, a position that she held until her death. She attended as many college functions and meetings as possible. At times, because of her precarious health, it was difficult for her to be active in meetings, but one trustee remembered that Jane's help in any endeavor was invaluable.

For Jane, activities also meant hobbies. She loved to make things with her hands. While coping with bouts of illness, sleepless nights, and restless days—and especially after her mother, Anna, died at the age of eighty-eight on November 20, 1962—she began to make "baubles" to keep her mind and hands busy. She fashioned pieces of old or broken costume jewelry into beautiful, glittering beaded ornaments that she gave to friends as Christmas presents. Although she could, and did, sell these ornaments to a New York City boutique, she was just as willing to donate them to a holiday craft fair that her church, Calvary Episcopal Church, held every year.

Flowers gave her great pleasure. In the winter, when the Missouri weather would not permit flowers to grow outside, Jane satisfied her green thumb by placing flower boxes in her bedroom window where they could get sunlight. She did the same thing when she was in the hospital for long periods of time. While Jane loved all flowers, one of her favorites was the petunia. She told a friend that it was a "lowly flower," not as

One of the many Christmas "baubles" that Jane made. (Photo by Ilene Stone; on display at the Boone County Historical Society and Museum, Columbia)

grand as a rose or an orchid, but that "no matter what you did to it, it came back." She cherished them because "they would grow in any weather, harsh weather—[and] still hold their heads up. [They] were very brave."

Those who knew Jane thought the same about her—that she was very brave. She was always coping with the consequences from her accident, such as injuries from falls, even though she took precautions. She used her crutches when going into situations she was unsure about and when she knew she might not have a companion's arm to rely upon for support. At other times, she used her cane for balance and because it indicated that she might need help.

Through it all, Jane remained as active and engaged with life as she could. She believed that activity was good therapy to keep her mind off of her problems. When it was not possible for her to go out, she busied herself with her "baubles," knitting, needlepoint, painting, reading, keeping up with current events, and gardening.

When people who knew Jane are asked what they remember most about her, the universal response is that she was always gracious. A fellow client at a Columbia beauty salon describes Jane as "very friendly . . . saying a few words to anyone. She did not know a stranger." In Jane's world, according to her friends, there were never any outsiders.

The former society editor of the *Columbia Daily Tribune,* Queen Smith, recalled that Jane was "a very bright girl." Dottie Benson came to the same conclusion. When asked what she remembered most about Jane, Dottie is quick to say that she "was sharp, she was so bright." She also recalls that she was a caring person, "just a good woman. [Her friends] thought she had suffered so much that it was refreshing to hear her laugh." Dottie's husband, Bob, remembers Jane as a "highly talented individual, a very special person, a great Missourian."

Another friend recalls Jane's incredible curiosity. Robert Broeg, a St. Louis newspaperman, remembers the "versatility of [her] conversation, her curiosity about my job as a well-traveled reporter, her theatrical and political observations and comments about sports." He recalls that Jane loved to talk; she would not allow her stuttering to stop her. She was a "chatterbox," Broeg recollects.

Her friends knew that Jane accepted the accolades that came her way with humility, thinking that what she was, and what she had done, was nothing special. The residents of Clinton, Missouri, where Jane spent some of her early years, thought differently. On July 25, 1973, the town honored Jane by proclaiming that date to be Jane Froman Day. The celebration was part of the twenty-fifth annual Henry County Fair, and included a reception, parade, dinner, and evening show. It was Jane's first visit back to her old hometown since 1936, and the whole town looked forward to visiting with her.

Jane's social life in Columbia included many special occasions. Here (left) *she attends a wedding reception on March 17, 1972. (Photo courtesy of Virginia Young)*

At the reception, the governor of Missouri, Christopher "Kit" Bond, teasingly lamented that he was not looking forward to sharing a stage with Jane because "she received most of the attention" from the huge crowd. For over an hour, she signed autographs and greeted fans. She later remarked that she was "so overwhelmed by such adoration that it was the most rewarding time" in her life, "second only to the USO tour" she made in 1945.

Three years later, the town honored her again. On July 29 in the bicentennial year of 1976, the location of the house where Jane Froman lived as a child was designated a historical site, and a marker was placed to identify it. Unfortunately, this time Jane could not be in Clinton to attend the ceremony. Smitty wrote to the Henry County Historical Society that Jane was "thrilled at her former home being selected for a special marker" but that she was "critically ill in February and March and underwent major surgery which kept her hospitalized for 42 days." She was now home, Smitty explained, but her condition was such that her doctors thought it would be August before she could travel. Jane had developed an abdominal problem that ultimately required surgery. During the operation, her heart had stopped. The doctors broke some of her ribs while restarting her heart, and the recovery from this crisis was a long one.

While Jane could not be there to personally thank the community of Clinton, she nevertheless wrote a warm and friendly letter to the town officials. She said that the ceremony was "an occasion I thoroughly hate to miss," and promised that when she was well enough she would "come to Clinton to see the old homeplace." She concluded by thanking those involved with the honor for helping her "recall my lovely childhood in Clinton. May it be equally as happy for the children of today and tomorrow. Love to you all!"

Jane never made it back to Clinton and never saw the marker at the site of her old house. In the remaining years of her life, travels outside her home were few.

16. *Beliefs and Good-bye*

In 1956, Jane Froman recorded an album of inspirational songs called *Faith*. One of the selections is entitled "One Little Candle." Some of the lyrics of this song reflect Jane's personal philosophy and seem a metaphor for certain aspects of her life, in particular, the words, "When the day is dark and dreary, and your way is hard to find," it is better to symbolically light "one little candle" than to dwell on misfortune or "stumble in the dark."

At the vulnerable age of five, Jane's way was indeed "hard to find." She was uprooted from the security of her home and moved to another town, in another part of Missouri. For unknown reasons, her beloved father had disappeared and her life was irrevocably changed.

Despite the kind words Jane wrote to the people of Clinton when they honored her by placing a marker at the site of her childhood home, her life there does not seem to have been particularly happy. Shortly after settling in Clinton she started to stutter, a difficulty that troubled her all her life. Her experiences at the convent and ridicule by her peers and others made for a bleak and isolating world for a young child. Jane could have permanently withdrawn and stumbled in the dark, but the discovery of her ability to sing and what she would later call her ancestors' "fighting spirits" saved her.

As an adult, when it seemed her career would provide her with stability, along came the devastating plane crash. By any standard, Jane's life was "dark and dreary" in 1943 and for years afterward. The severe and permanent injuries she sustained, physical and emotional, would have broken many peo-

Cover from the sheet music of "I Believe." (From the collection of Michael Modero. Copyright permission granted by the Richmond Organization)

ple. They almost crushed Jane. One close friend of hers said, "You just cannot get away from the fact that she was strong."

Jane did not plan for her life to become a symbol of courage and inspiration to others. She never intended to be a champion of causes for those who were on the outside of society. However, she knew what it was like to be slighted, and when confronted with similar situations she did not shy away from them. Whether it was a person who could not attend a performance she was giving because of the color of his skin, or a child or adult with physical or emotional problems, or some worthy cause that needed the attention that only celebrity could bring, Jane was there. In her support of others she was ahead of her time in many ways.

This is not to suggest that Jane was a Pollyanna. There were outbursts of anger, feelings of frustration, and many moments of despair. There were poignant times when the past came flooding back. Another close friend once innocently remarked that her relatives had spent some time in the Azores. In response, Jane wistfully remembered, "That was the last place that I walked on two good feet." The Azores was the last refueling stop that the *Yankee Clipper* made before it crashed into the Tagus River. For the most part, though, there was no dwelling on the past.

Those who knew Jane admired, respected, and were often in awe of her, wondering from where her inner strength came. Her second husband, John Burn, explained it most eloquently when he added a postscript to the script for *With a Song in My Heart.*

It would seem as though every possible obstacle were interposed between the girl and the thing she sought to attain, as though she were being submitted to a trial, infinite in its severity. She accepted such conditions; further, she imposed the strictest of ethics on herself. She must fight all times honorably, ask little of others, and at the same time fulfill every obligation in a fuller measure than is asked of those not so burdened as she. I think you may search back through the years . . . and never find [such] an example of humanity at its best.

There came a time, however, when Jane's stubbornness of character, her own fighting spirit, could not overcome the effects of her latest injury. On Christmas Eve 1979, Jane and Smitty were on their way to a holiday party. Smitty was driving and Jane was sitting next to him in the front seat. As they were turning into the driveway of their friend's house, an oncoming car slammed into their vehicle. Stunned but not seriously hurt, Smitty was able to get out of the car. Jane was not so lucky. She received the direct impact of the collision, and she was trapped in the car until rescue workers were able to free her. Badly shaken and with minor injuries, Jane spent some time in the hospital because of her frail health. In the past, she had always seemed to bounce back when her physical condition faltered. Not this time.

On April 22, 1980, Jane was at home by herself. Since she disliked talking on the phone, she and Smitty had devised a special telephone code so that he could check on her. Smitty would call home, let the phone ring two times, and then hang up. He would then immediately call back. She would know it was Smitty and answer the phone. This is what he probably did on that Tuesday afternoon. The phone rang twice; he hung up and dialed again. No one responded. Concerned for Jane, Smitty hurried home and went to her bedroom. He found her in bed. Jane had passed away.

Smitty ran out of the house to seek help. He found a teenaged neighbor and asked the young man to assist him. They returned to the house and made the necessary phone calls. Jane's certificate of death states that she died of cardiac arrest due to chronic heart and lung disease. The heart that was filled with thousands of songs and the captivating voice that had shared them with the world were stilled. She was seventy-two years old.

Jane's funeral was held three days later. People jammed the small Episcopal church where Jane had worshipped; they came from everywhere to say their good-byes. There were dignitaries, friends from all parts of the country, and friends

Resolution

WHEREAS, the members of the Senate of the Eightieth General Assembly of the State of Missouri are deeply saddened to learn that a valiant heart is forever stilled, Jane Froman Smith is dead; and

WHEREAS, Jane Froman will be forever enshrined as one of America's great popular song stylists and she will also forever be remembered as a warm and loving unique human being; and

WHEREAS, born in University City, Missouri, she spent most of her formative years in Columbia, Missouri, graduating from the University of Missouri in 1928; and

WHEREAS, she began her singing career at the age of eight and went on to perform in the 1933 edition of the Ziegfeld Follies; later she gained fame with performances on the NBC Radio Network, in nightclubs and with Paul Whiteman's Orchestra; and

WHEREAS, with the beginning of World War II, Miss Froman devoted her time and talents to the entertainment of American Servicemen around the world and fast became one of the troops' favorite entertainers; and

WHEREAS, during one of these trips, Miss Froman was involved in a tragic airplane crash and spent three of the next five years in hospitals enduring twenty-five operations on her legs; and

WHEREAS, despite her severe injuries, Miss Froman made an astounding comeback and was eventually able to walk without crutches, going on to star on Broadway and keeping her engagements with servicemen, touring and performing for over 300,000 troups; and

WHEREAS, in later years she appeared in leading television programs, including her own "Jane Froman Show" and her life story was the subject of a motion picture "With a Song in My Heart"; and

WHEREAS, not only did she have a song in her heart, but love and kindness also abided there and every person who was privileged to know her has keen memories of a great lady who truly saw the beauty of living and lived that beauty to the fullest in her own life; and

WHEREAS, it is with a great sadness in our hearts, with great love and warmth in our memories of her, and with great thanks to a loving God for giving her to us for this short while, that we bid a last fond farewell to Jane Froman Smith;

NOW, THEREFORE, BE IT RESOLVED that the members of the Senate pause in their legislative deliberations to pay tribute to her memory, to extend their sincere condolences to her husband, Mr. Rowland Smith, and to those who knew and loved her on their irreplaceable loss, and to try to express in all too inadequate words the sense of love and of loss that all Missourians feel on her passing; and

BE IT FURTHER RESOLVED that the Secretary of the Senate be instructed to send a properly inscribed copy of this resolution to Mr. Rowland Smith, Columbia, Missouri.

Offered by Senator Roger Wilson

STATE OF MISSOURI:
CITY OF JEFFERSON:
                              :ss
SENATE CHAMBER   :

I, Norman L. Merrell, President Pro Tem of the Senate, do hereby certify the above and foregoing to be a full, true and complete copy of Senate Resolution No. 614, offered into and adopted on April 23, 1980, as fully as the same appears of record.

IN TESTIMONY WHEREOF, I have hereunto set my hand and affixed the seal of the Senate of the State of Missouri this 23rd day of April, A.D. 1980.

Norman L. Merrell
PRESIDENT PRO TEM
80TH GENERAL ASSEMBLY

On April 23, 1980, the day after Jane's death, the Missouri State Senate passed a resolution honoring her and observed a moment of silence in her memory. (Columbia College)

from her beloved city of Columbia. Her white casket was covered with pink roses. The funeral service, about an hour long, disappointed some of her friends because there was little mention of her contributions and accomplishments. At the conclusion of the service, Jane was buried at the Columbia Cemetery. Placed with her was a small gold cross that she had always kept by her bed. It was her only possession that was recovered from the 1943 plane crash.

In his 1993 book *Lawyers and the American Dream,* Stuart M. Speiser, one of Jane's attorneys in her case against Pan American Airways, details the events of the trial in several chapters. Speiser states that upon her death, Jane was released "from a tortured existence." It is true that the last four years of Jane's life, especially the months after the car accident, were more difficult for her, if that is possible, than the years that preceded them. It is equally true, according to those who knew her, that Jane did not consider her life to be "tortured." She took her life, pain and all, and made a meaningful contribution to others. All the people that she touched, either by knowing her or hearing her sing, were better off for the experience. If Jane's years in show business after the plane crash and her years of retirement in Columbia are characterized merely as a "tortured existence," then all that she achieved is diminished.

Difficult though it was for Jane, her contributions to others were significant, and they in turn enhanced her existence. One acquaintance thought she should be remembered not only for having a song in her heart, but "a smile on her face." A long-time friend recalled that "Jane was my education" because she "shared so much, so many ideas, thoughts, and experiences." Another remarked on Jane's great empathy, which "made you feel comfortable, at ease," remembering that she looked directly at you because she was "extremely interested in what you had to say . . . she was interested in people."

Jane had no illusions about her life once she made up her

On May 27, 1996, the Boone County Historical Society designated the Columbia Cemetery as an historic site. As part of the events that day, the society selected Jane's grave and those of other prominent people for special recognition. (Photo by Ilene Stone)

mind to retire in Columbia. She came back in 1961 to rebuild her health, as much as it could be restored. She enrolled at the University of Missouri to take art classes and became an honor student. She renewed an old friendship that blossomed into marriage. Her life changed. As she wrote, "the adventure of the rich, full life of homemaking, like every other woman in the town," was now hers. She enriched her days with activities that brought her satisfaction and accomplishments. At the heart of it all, though, was the knowledge that she had done the right thing by leaving show business. Jane acknowledged in her autobiography that she drew comfort from the fact that she was "Home now, home forever, and oh Thank God, humbly and gratefully, for giving me the understanding and the wisdom to find my way when it was time to go home."

EPILOGUE *The Two Janes*

Throughout their lives, people show different sides of themselves. There is the public person, the one who meets and greets people, who must meet certain expectations. Then there is a private side, where individuals can be themselves, with no pretenses. Certainly, there were two different Janes. One Jane was the star that audiences and critics adored. The other Jane was a private person—the one whom few people ever saw. Each Jane dealt with her own feelings and emotions, but each intertwined with the other.

The public Jane was the entertainer, the singer with one of the most extraordinary voices of her time. It was this Jane that thousands, during her long career, came to hear sing, listened to on radio or records, and watched on television. She had what was described, time and time again, as "the Froman presence." Head held high, shoulders back, and chin out, she looked taller than her five-foot, six-inch frame. She swept into a room or onto a stage, leaving no doubt that she had arrived at her destination. This was the entertainer who pioneered the use of the handheld microphone, which permitted her to move about the stage as she sang. It is a technique that most stage artists use today, although now the microphone is often cordless or worn as a headset.

After the plane crash, Jane the performer covered up the badges of honor she had earned in 1943. There were floor-length dresses to hide the brace on her right leg. Jane always wore either long-sleeved gowns, gloves reaching to the elbow, or a shawl that covered the awful scarring of her right forearm, which ran from her wrist to her elbow. She learned to walk with a glide-step to disguise the limp she had because her right leg was an inch and a half shorter than her left. No matter that this technique would eventually contribute to her back problems. She was the public Jane—performer par excellence. This Jane was a star, and stars must be perfect in every way.

Jane the entertainer became the symbol of tremendous courage, determination, and grit. She was the person who never cried, who never displayed a temper, who was never depressed. None of these emotions were seen by the public. She was the person who just kept going, no matter what life threw in her way. When Jane performed, there was no hint of the turmoil that she faced each day. All that people saw was "Jane Froman," beautifully coiffed, dressed in designer gowns, and wearing elegant jewelry, singing the songs of the best composers of the day. That was the way she wanted to be seen when she entertained.

However, there was another Jane, a more private Jane. In many ways, this Jane was more human and more real. When Jane was not on stage, when she was not before an audience, when she was giving interviews or doing charity work, she made no attempt to hide her disabilities, and was always kind and gracious. It was the private Jane, however, who was left to deal with the consequences of those disabilities.

When Jane the entertainer visited Walter Reed Army Hospital in Washington, D.C., in November 1953, she made light of the fact that the "private Jane" could not walk from the hospital's radio station—where she sang to the patients throughout the hospital—to a far-off ward that she was to visit. Since the distance was too great for her to walk comfortably, the hospital provided a wheelchair. In November 1969, when Jane visited a veterans hospital in Kansas City, Missouri, to cheer up the patients, she slipped and fell. The public Jane laughed off the incident with a joke about "nonskid wax floors." But it took the private Jane a long time to recover from that mishap.

The public never knew of her continuing need for psychi-

Jane is one of the relatively few celebrities to have more than two stars on the Hollywood Walk of Fame. She has one for her work on radio, one for recordings, and one for television. The stars were placed when the walk opened on February 2, 1960. (Photos by Raluca Hirina, Claudia Sandoval, Hallie Stone)

atric help long after her stay at the Menninger Clinic. As Jane the singer continued performing, the private Jane saw a prominent New York psychiatrist as her marriage to John Burn was ending. Publicly, people believed that Jane was fine. In reality, she was dealing with a great deal of heartache. In the late 1950s, when poor health, back surgeries, and a long-lasting and profound fear of going back on the stage forced Jane the performer to put her career on hold once more, it was the private Jane who again sought help from her New York psychiatrist.

Out of the limelight, Jane could show flashes of anger and frustration. In her unfinished autobiography, she reveals that she had a temper along with her strong will. She bit the piano at the convent when she was a child, angry at having to practice hour after hour when she already knew how to play. Then there is the story that during one of her numerous hospital stays after she retired, she threw a glass out the door of her room into the hallway, almost hitting a passerby. After that incident, a note was put on her chart that Mrs. Smith was allowed only plastic glasses. Such flare-ups of irritation and even rage were directed at those closest to her—her family, friends, or staff. Only they saw these outbursts.

It is understandable that there were times when the circumstances of Jane's life became overwhelming. Jane wrote, in notes for the film about her life, that she "learned long ago that all the tears, all the Oh, no, no, God wouldn't let this happen to me, doesn't change the fact that you wake up in the morning and there it is." She was the first to admit that when she returned home from Portugal in April 1943 and saw such simple things as a glass of milk and a piece of white bread, "the furies [took] possession of my soul."

Those furies never left. In 1959 Jane applied for a scholarship from an art school that taught classes by mail. The application, found in the Froman Papers at the Western Historical Manuscript Collection, asked her to list her goals in life. Jane wrote the following: "To be an outgoing, constructive, active productive person." It was as if all that she had accomplished, before and after the *Yankee Clipper* plunged into the Tagus River, had no significance. The furies were still there.

From 1943 on, Jane constantly fought osteomyelitis, arthritis, falls, back pain, pain from her brace, headaches, lung and abdominal problems, hospitalizations, surgeries, depression, and more. And she still had to cope with her stuttering. As Jane battled to face each day, she thought of the discomfort that she experienced in terms of colors. As she described them in her film notes, "brown [was] a deep and steady pain" and there was a "bright green pain [that] was a shock—a zip." She could have given up and quit at any time, but she did not. She often told others that "when you get to the end of your rope, tie a knot and hang on." This saying may not be original to Jane, but it is symbolic of what she did.

Jane Froman had humanity, gallantry, and stubbornness. She had a fighting spirit. Such qualities brought back a career she thought she had lost forever in 1943, and they permitted her to do all that she did for others, before and after her retirement. The private Jane fought the furies in her soul, thus allowing the world to know, respect, and admire the public Jane. This was Jane Froman—Missouri's, and America's, first lady of song.

This portrait of Jane hangs in the Jane Froman Room of the Memorial Union on the campus of the University of Missouri–Columbia. In the room are other pictures of Jane, including one on the cover of LIFE magazine, March 14, 1938. (Photo by Carol Kennedy)

For More Reading, Listening, and Viewing

The following list contains sources of information on Jane Froman's life and work and other selected resource materials that can be found in any major library.

PRIMARY SOURCE MATERIAL

The Jane Froman Papers are located at the Western Historical Manuscript Collection at the University of Missouri–Columbia. The papers consist of correspondence, financial records, sheet music arrangements, photographs, scrapbooks (on microfilm), and cassettes and videotapes of Jane's television shows. Jane's husband, Rowland H. Smith, donated these documents to the archives in August 1980.

The Jane Froman Collection, housed at the Western Historical Manuscript Collection as well, contains recordings of performances and interviews that Jane gave over the course of her long career, assembled from donations by friends and researchers.

Columbia College's collection of Jane Froman memorabilia, while not as extensive as the above-mentioned collections, has many written materials (including Jane's notes for her unpublished autobiography), photographs, awards that she received over the years, and many of the gowns and dresses that belonged to her.

The Boone County Historical Society/Walters–Boone County Historical Museum has a smaller collection of Froman memorabilia. On display are photographs, sheet music, movie lobby cards, playbills, and other items related to Jane, including one of the "baubles" she made. The exhibit also has an audio system that allows visitors to hear Jane sing.

SECONDARY SOURCE MATERIAL
Books

Lawyers and the American Dream, by Stuart M. Speiser (New York: Evans and Company, 1993), devotes several chapters to Jane and her struggles after the 1943 plane crash, with special attention to her lawsuit against Pan American Airways. This account is especially informative since the author was one of Jane's attorneys.

Red: The Tempestuous Life of Susan Hayward, by Robert La Guardia and Gene Arceri (New York: Macmillan, 1985), contains information about Susan and Jane during the filming of *With a Song in My Heart.*

Susan Hayward: Portrait of a Survivor, by Beverly Linet (New York: Atheneum, 1980), like *Red,* provides insight into the filming of Jane's life story.

Government Publications

Congressional Record. 82d Cong., 2d sess., April 9, 1952. Appendix, A2298. Resolution recognizing Jane Froman.

Missouri State Senate. Resolution honoring Jane Froman Smith. April 23, 1980.

Periodicals

"A Child Singing," by Jane Froman, *Parade* (March 27, 1960), recounts how Jane found her way back to performing after medical setbacks in the late 1950s.

"Across Our Wide Missouri, Jane Froman: With a Song in Her Heart," by Bob Priddy, *Missouri Life* (July–August 1980), features a narrative of Jane's life and pays tribute to her accomplishments.

"A Magic Moment: Jane Froman Sings Again," by Henry J.

Waters III, *Columbia Daily Tribune* (December 22, 1969), is a review of Jane's Christmas concert at Arrow Rock, Missouri—her first solo performance in nine years.

"As Nice as Folks Remembered," *Columbia Missourian* (February 21, 1962), is an editorial remarking on Jane's return to Columbia.

"Aunt Jane, With Love," by Deena Meiner, *Missouri Life* (September–October 1983) is a memoir written by one of Jane's young fans who went on to become a lifelong friend.

"Clinton Parish Celebrates 100 Years of Rich History," by John Ratterman, *Catholic KEY* (October 19, 1975), recounts the history of the Holy Rosary Academy.

"Crash Proved Paradoxical Blessing for Jane Froman," *Los Angeles Times* (April 28, 1980), is an obituary that tells how Jane's stay at the Menninger Clinic changed her life.

"Jane," by Peggy Phillips, *Christian College Magazine* (April 1962), describes how Jane adjusted to life back in Columbia when she took art classes at the University of Missouri.

"Jane Froman: After 9 Years She Sings Again," by Bob M. Gassaway, *Columbia Daily Tribune* (December 19, 1969), tells of Jane's decision to sing again at Arrow Rock and her preparation for the event.

"Jane Froman: Courage Unlimited," by Isabella Taves, *McCall's* (May 1952), is one of the better accounts of Jane's life, career, and marriages up to the date it was written.

"She Lived My Life," by Jane Froman, *Photoplay* (July 1952), relates how Susan Hayward "became" Jane for the movie *With a Song in My Heart.*

"Singing Girl," by Kyle Chrichton, *Collier's* (February 29, 1936), details events in Jane's early career.

"Song in Her Heart," by Arthur Mann, *Collier's* (January 22, 1944), is an article about Jane's survival of the plane crash and her return to performing in *Artists and Models.*

"The Woman I Have Become," by Jane Froman, *Good Housekeeping* (November 1952), is a thoughtful account of Jane's inner feelings about how her life changed after 1943.

There are many more magazine and newspaper items, too numerous to note, regarding Jane Froman. The two rolls of microfilm in the Jane Froman Papers contain countless articles saved by a clipping service, in addition to those gathered by family and friends. *The Readers' Guide,* found in any library, lists stories about Jane that appeared in various periodicals throughout her life.

Recordings

Copies of Jane's records can be found in stores that sell old recordings and on auction sites on the Internet. Over the last few years, some of Jane's recordings have been rereleased on compact discs and they are available in record stores and on the Internet. Here is a partial list of CDs:

Jane Froman: My Heart Speaks. Jasmine Music, 1998.
Jane Froman on Capitol. Capitol Music Special Markets for Collectors' Choice Music, 1996.
Jane Froman: Songs at Sunset/Faith: Original Recordings from 1952–1957. Encore Productions, 1999.
Jane Froman: The Star thru Three Decades. Encore Productions, 1994.
Jane Froman: With a Song in My Heart. EMI—Capitol Music Special Markets for Good Music Record Company, 1996.

Films

None of Jane's films are available for purchase on video or DVD. However, the cable television stations American Movie Classics (AMC) and Turner Classic Movies (TCM) occasionally show her films. Here is a listing of Jane's movies:

Kissing Time. Warner Brothers, 1933.
Radio City Revels. RKO, 1938.
Stars over Broadway. Warner Brothers, 1935.
With a Song in My Heart. Twentieth Century Fox, 1952.

Copies of these films can often be found for sale on Internet sites. The Boone County Historical Society and Museum has *Kissing Time* on permanent loan from Turner Broadcasting.

Television and Radio Programs

The Jane Froman Papers at the Western Historical Manuscript Collection has four broadcasts of *The Jane Froman Show* from 1955. Each is fifteen minutes long. The Jane Froman Collection has one copy of Jane's television show *USA Canteen*. This program, thirty minutes long, aired on October 25, 1952. The Western Historical Manuscript Collection also has a wide range of audiotapes from radio and television shows on which Jane appeared.

The Boone County Historical Society and Museum has a 1955 copy of *The Jimmy Durante Show: The Gala Twenty-fifth Anniversary Show* on permanent loan. Jane is the only guest on this thirty-minute program, in which she sings, dances, and does comedy routines with Durante.

With locations in New York and Los Angeles, the Museum of Television and Radio has in its archives several television shows from the 1950s that feature Jane.

Web Sites

With the growth of the Internet, Web sites with information about Jane have appeared. Using a search engine and typing in "Jane Froman" will give a listing of these sites.

Index

Page numbers in italics refer to photos and photo captions.

About the Author

Ilene Stone became interested in Jane Froman in 1994 when she saw the movie With a Song in My Heart. *In 1997 she coauthored* One Little Candle: Remembering Jane Froman, *an account of Froman's retirement years. Stone was an adjunct faculty member in American history at San Diego Community College, where she taught for more than thirty years. She currently resides in Spring Valley, California. (Photo by Jeff Stone)*